Praise for

Rob Durant and The Social Enablement Blueprint

"The world doesn't need to scale sales. It needs to scale relationships."

- Mark Shaefer

Top Voice in Personal Branding, and author of *Belonging to the Brand*

"In 'Social Enablement,' Rob masterfully explores the transformative power of social connections in the modern world and the applications to the growing and maturing field of enablement. This book is a compelling guide to harnessing the potential of our networks, fostering meaningful relationships, and driving collective success. How you think about and execute selling will never be the same. Rob's insights are not just timely but essential for anyone looking to thrive and win in an interconnected society."

-Jill Guardia

SVP Revenue Enablement & Operations, Thought Industries

THE SOCIAL ENABLEMENT BLUEPRINT

Effective selling requires personal connection. Yet, for the most part, technology increasingly gets in the way of people authentically engaging with one another. In his book, Rob details how motivated individuals can leverage technology to:

- Be **approachable**, establishing a social presence that reflects one's true self... creating the foundation for building meaningful relationships

- Be **sociable**, engaging actively with one's network by participating in conversations, sharing insights and showing genuine interest in others... fostering real interactions

- Be **generous**, sharing insights and offers of help freely, building trust... positioning oneself as a valuable resource

Even as expectations of AI-powered interactions reach new heights, those who follow Rob's three key recommendations will be rewarded with stronger, more mutually satisfying relationships and better business results.

It's about time this book was written. Congratulations, and thank you, Rob!

-Lee Levitt
Principal, Acelera Group

PRAISE FOR

"Having had the opportunity to work closely with Rob, I can attest to his insightful sales approach and unwavering drive. Rob's ability to blend practical strategies with industry knowledge has not only earned him respect in academia but also among top sales leaders. The approach detailed in this book is transformative, making the guidance invaluable for anyone looking to excel in modern sales."

- Andrew Hough FF.ISP
Founder & Director, Institute of Sales Professionals,
and Lecturer, Cranfield School of Management

"You will leave any interaction with Rob understanding the value of relationships. Through his teachings and unique style, you'll understand how to enable yourself, your sales teams, and your company as to why social selling is a must-have strategy."

- Greg Wasserman
Podcast Coach & Consultant, Time & Relationships Consulting,
and Head of Relationships, Castmagic

"Rob has a way of turning sales into genuine connections, making you realize it's more about relationships than just closing deals."

- Alyssa Nolte
CEO of TruVue

THE SOCIAL ENABLEMENT BLUEPRINT

"Rob completely shifted our mindset on how to be effective in the modern era of connectivity. And once you understand the shift, it all becomes so simple, motivating, and achievable to execute on. We're completely bought in to social enablement as a sales technique."

- Bryce Tully
CEO, innerlogic

"Rob's teaching and presenting style is dynamic and highly impactful. His ability to guide Founders on leveraging social media is invaluable, providing practical and effective strategies that have yielded significant results for us."

-Michael Bawol
President, innerlogic

"Rob Durant puts the 'social' back into social media. His dynamic teaching style focuses on the importance of leveraging social media with three key principles: Be Approachable, Be Sociable, and Be Generous. Rob truly lives these principles in his business and relationships, showing that sales is about building real, meaningful connections, not just transactions. If you aren't sure this can work or is for you and your business, just have a conversation with Rob!"

- Donna Kunde
Global Radio Authority & Podcast Expert
Co-Author of THE INFLUENCERS FORMULA

The Social Enablement Blueprint

Stop Pitching! START SELLING

Rob Durant

Flywheel Results LLC

Thank you to

my wife,

my children,

Mom & Dad, and the rest of my family.

You have always been there to support me.

Thank you also to Tim Hughes & Adam Gray

and the many DLA Ignite associates –

people I consider friends, not just colleagues.

Foreword by Tim Hughes

Had this been 10 years ago, Rob would have never asked me to write the forward to his book. We would have never met; he lives 3,271 miles away from me. Sorry to be precise but I looked it up on Google. Rob lives in Boston in the USA and I live in London in the UK.

Our lives would never have met.

But we have the internet and social media to thank for us meeting. Since the internet's creation, there is now two thirds of the world's population connected and there is sixty-two percent of the world's population active on social media. And by-the-way, active means the average person spends two hours twenty minutes a day on social media. I looked that up on Google, as well.

The internet and social media have offered to the world a massive opportunity to meet, to have conversations, and exchange ideas. Some of these conversations turn into sales, some of these conversations turn into working together and what I hope is a life-long friendship.

But while you are reading this and you are thinking "I know this", the problem is, you have -and I'm pretty sure about this - done nothing to empower your C-Suite, your sales people, your human resources people, in fact the whole of your employees to take advantage of these benefits.

Even though the data clearly shows you will get more pipeline, more revenue, access to a better talent pool, better investors all at a lower cost.

What Rob has done with this book is peel back the curtain on some of these business advantages, especially for your salespeople. He's done this, not with a fire hose of information, but in a step by step way that will enable you time to absorb and understand the changes that have taken place.

Tim Hughes, Co-Founder and CEO of DLA Ignite

"Should have Played Quidditch for England"

Foreword by Adam Gray

If you work in enablement you absolutely have to read this book. It is a step-by-step guide to how you can bring sales and enablement kicking and screaming into the 21st century.

For too long enablement has focused on adding efficiencies to, and enabling people to use software based on, the broken premise that if you - send more emails, make more phone calls, choose better words - somehow you will be able to generate more opportunities. Sadly, particularly since Covid, this hasn't been the case.

The entire enablement function needs to be reimagined to reflect not just current trends and technologies but more importantly current customer buying behaviours.

When buyers increasingly seek a rep-free buying experience how can the rep engage them and influence the decisions that they make? They certainly can't do this through sending emails called calling and having a sales focused approach. Instead salespeople need to put relationships front and centre of what they're trying to achieve.

What is really interesting is that this concepts discussed are not groundbreaking. Everybody knows that they need to make the customer the focus of what they do, however the abstract concept of a customer centric view of a business's activities and the concrete actions that departments need to take are worlds apart. Crystallising these abstract ideas into a series of straightforward repeatable actionable insights is often missing from most strategies.

This book connects those dots. It doesn't lead the enablement function by the nose to a solution but what it does do is it encourages enablement to see their role as more than implementors of software or trainers of sales methodologies and allows enablement departments to truly provide value to their organisations. This value can best be articulated as "helping to dig the organisation out of the hole in which they find themselves", a hole in which every organisation finds itself - a shortfall of revenue, a shortfall of pipeline and, perhaps more worrying, no reliable mechanism for generating more pipeline. This is the solution for every organisation has been looking.

What Rob is able to do is give the enablement department the blueprint they need to navigate revops once more to safe waters.

Adam Gray is the Co-Founder of DLA Ignite

"For fun I sometimes play the guitar..."

Preface

It was a problem I didn't exactly know I had.

It was a solution I didn't know existed.

What is Social Enablement?

Social Enablement is the process by which salespeople leverage social media to drive more conversations and ultimately drive more opportunity.

Social Enablement is also the process by which organizational Leaders, Enablement, Marketing, and HR professionals can support the Sales Team – *enable* them, as it were – in their social efforts.

What is IGNITE?

The IGNITE methodology is a comprehensive program designed to empower sales professionals and organizations to leverage social media platforms effectively. It provides both a strategic and tactical approach for individuals and organizations to leverage social media to drive more conversations and ultimately drive more opportunity. Unlike traditional sales methods, IGNITE focuses on enhancing visibility, building genuine relationships, and positioning sales teams as trusted advisors through a structured approach.

I'm not a "guru" or a "ninja" or a "capital 'I' Influencer". I am someone who wants to help, guide, and mentor. At my core, I am a teacher.

I've been a teacher and sales trainer for over 20 years now.

I started my career with the Walt Disney Company, then I worked for Verizon for just over a decade. Most recently I've helped build and scale sales teams for three different start-ups as their first Sales Enablement hire. Each has gone on to become a unicorn.

At the core of what I teach is direct from Simon Sinek's, "Start with Why". I teach my students to create very carefully crafted audience-centric emails and voicemails that speak to why.

But lately what I was teaching was not working. Sales reps were not getting the kind of response we were accustomed to getting.

"Maybe it's me," I thought. Maybe my messaging is off. Maybe my methods are outdated. But as we will see in this book, it wasn't just my teaching methods; industry research proves this is a down-trend across the board.

We heard from a lot sales teams recently, "If what we've always been doing doesn't work anymore how can we sell?" They have to sell. Nothing happens for an organization until a sale is made.

Then I met Tim Hughes. Tim is the Co-Founder and CEO of DLA and the best-selling author of **Social Selling: Techniques to Influence Buyers and Changemakers**. Tim is also recognized as the most influential social seller in the world. After hearing what he had to say I figured out how I can help salespeople going forward. I was glad to be invited to be a DLA Associate.

What I learned was that up to this point I had been practicing random acts of social behavior – an occasional comment here, and maybe, if I was feeling particularly brave, I'd post something. It was part of the 98% of LinkedIn users who read but don't post. I mean, even if I did post something, who would want to read it, right?

It turns out there is an audience for you out there. DLA Ignite has developed an over-arching social selling methodology, the IGNITE Social Selling and Influence sales methodology, along with the prescriptive steps you need to take at each step of the way.

It's the simple 3-step process of IGNITE that I want to share with you in this book:

1. Be Approachable

2. Be Sociable

3. Be Generous

In addition, I will share ways organizational Leaders, Enablement, Marketing, and HR can support Sales Teams in their efforts to leverage social media to drive more conversations and ultimately drive more opportunity.

In other words, this book is intended to serve as a blueprint for enabling salespeople to be effective at being social.

About the Author

At my core, I am a teacher.

I'm the son of a math teacher. My Dad has taught in public schools for over 50 years! Even in his retirement he still teaches at a local community college.

But when it came time for me to go to college he strongly discouraged me from going into teaching. He told me it was difficult to raise a family as a teacher. I saw his struggles and understood.

Instead I went into business. But in every role I found myself gravitating towards helping, mentoring, leading, training - Teaching.

I started my career with the Walt Disney Company, the company credited with inventing the field of customer service. There I learned the art & science of providing outstanding customer service. But when it came time for me to raise a family of my own it was important for us to be closer to our extended family and we moved back to Boston.

Eventually I landed with the phone company. After weeks of interviews and batteries of tests I still remember the call from the HR representative, "Rob, we'd like to offer you the role of customer service representative. But please know, there is a sales quota with this role."

Ugh. I swallowed hard and took the job. But up to this point I had the same (mis)perception about sales that many I encounter in customer service today still have: Sales is EVIL! Sales is yucky. If Sales didn't screw up somewhere we wouldn't NEED customer service!

I have since come to learn I could not have been more wrong. Eventually I became a highly successful sales representative – bonuses, prizes, Presidents Club trips and all that.

But my true nature is helping, mentoring, guiding. While I could help one customer at a time as a sales rep, I saw my impact scale as I helped others do the same. Eventually I transitioned into sales leadership, sales training, sales operations, and what is now known as Sales Enablement, and more recently Revenue Enablement. Let's just call it "Enablement".

At one point in my career I had an opportunity to teach in public high schools - and loved every minute of it. My Dad was right - it was difficult to raise a family as a teacher, but we got by somehow.

But when the start-up world reached out to me and said, "Rob, we want you to help our sales team get from point A to point Z. Not only do we not have the roads built, we haven't drawn the map!" I jumped at the chance.

I LOVE working with start-ups! The fast pace, the green field to develop new things, the younger generation I get to mentor and help build their career foundations - this is EXCITING to me!

One of the great things about working for startups is you never hear, "That's not the way we do things around here." Mostly because they haven't done it yet.

One of the challenges about working for startups is having to pivot. As their first Enablement hire, I've helped three different startups achieve unicorn status. But once through hyper-growth, they decided to pivot away from devoting full-time resources to enablement.

With that, I ventured off on my own. Through my company, Flywheel Results, I get to work with a myriad of companies - tech and otherwise. I serve as a mentor coaching with various incubators. And I've even had the opportunity to get back into teaching as an Adjunct at a local university.

I found my calling. I help to build organizations by building the careers of those who join them. By teaching.

Writing a book isn't easy

Sure, it's easy enough to know what you want to say, but sometimes saying it can be challenging. And sometimes just finding the time to say what you want to say can be difficult.

More than once I thought about quitting.

Then I heard the words I needed to hear –

"HOW DARE YOU!"

How dare you keep this to yourself when you know the benefits it brings!

How dare you keep this to yourself when you know how much small businesses are suffering.

How dare you keep this to yourself when you know how many salespeople are struggling to meet their quotas, and the companies that are relying on them are going under.

How dare you keep this to yourself when you know how hard it is for non-profits to bring awareness to their cause!

How dare you keep this to yourself when you personally know the pain, fear, and struggles of wearing the "Open to Work" banner?

How dare you, sir?

HOW DARE YOU!

This book is the culmination of gifts so many have generously given me. In that spirit, my hope is that it provides some benefit to you.

Contents

Chapter One

Why This Book?

Why now?

"Nothing happens until a sale is made."

It's clear to many of us in sales -

Traditional sales methods are becoming less effective.

Cold calls, cold emails, and advertising response rates, once the pillars of sales and marketing strategies, are yielding diminishing returns - and have been for a while. Sales reps are facing historically low engagement rates with their outreach efforts, and the methods that once guaranteed responses are no longer delivering the same results. Quotas are being missed. *Jobs are on the line!*

In 2020 the sales industry (and the world) changed dramatically. With the sudden and extreme transfer to virtual selling, we heard from a lot of sales teams, "If what we've always been doing doesn't work anymore how can we sell?"

Automation can help, right? Well, doing MORE of something that doesn't work... doesn't work.

AI can help, right? There are some things AI can help with, but it turns out in the short time we've been exposed to AI people can recognize when AI is being used to "personalize" messages – and they don't much care for it.

But salespeople have to sell. Nothing happens until a sale is made.

> **"Nothing happens until a sale is made."**
> **– Thomas Watson Sr.**

Originally attributed to Thomas Watson Sr., former president of IBM, this statement has been part of the business world for over seventy years. It underscores a fundamental truth in business: Sales are the lifeblood of any organization. Without sales, there is no revenue, and without revenue, a company cannot sustain itself. This principle was the impetus for and the bedrock upon which the IGNITE Social Selling & Influence sales methodology was built more than 7 years ago.

An urgent need for a new approach to sales was needed, one that aligned with the changing behaviors of buyers. As we will see in **THE STATE OF THE INDUSTRY FOR SALES AND MARKETING**, the modern buyer's journey has evolved dramatically. It's time for the seller's journey to evolve in kind.

As salespeople, we have to sell; and to do so effectively, we have to adapt to the way people want to buy. The traditional sales pitch is no longer enough. In today's world, success in sales requires building relationships, establishing trust, and providing value long before a sales conversation begins.

This book introduces a new concept - **Social Enablement**. Leveraging the IGNITE Social Selling & Influence methodology, this book explains how Sales and Organizational Leaders, Sales Enablement, Marketing, and HR/ Learning & Development can support Sales Teams in their quest to develop a digital-first, buyer-centric approach to sales. This approach transforms how salespeople - and entire organizations - can connect with, engage with, and support their prospects and clients by leveraging their personal social media presence.

The genesis of this book is closely tied to the development and delivery of the IGNITE Social Selling & Influence program. The course was designed to address the shortcomings of traditional sales training by focusing on the skills and strategies needed to succeed in a digital-first, socially connected world. It teaches sales professionals how to build a strong personal brand, engage effectively on social media, and create content that resonates with their audience. However, unlike other social selling programs, this is not a typical connect-and-pitch approach to social media.

This book aims to equip salespeople with the tools and knowledge necessary to move from outdated sales tactics to a more sophisticated, relationship-driven approach. It also seeks to enable those who support them. By doing so, salespeople can not only survive but thrive in an environment where the buyer holds more power than ever before.

In essence, **The Social Enablement Blueprint: Stop Pitching! START SELLING** is more than an explanation of a sales methodology. It's a call to action for sales professionals - and entire organizations - to embrace change, adopt new strategies, and ultimately become more effective and successful in their roles. Because, at the end of the day, while many things in business may change, the truth remains: **Nothing happens until a sale is made.**

We're all in Sales

In his book **To Sell is Human**, Dan Pink explores the nature of sales in the modern era. Pink argues that traditional views of sales as merely the domain of slick, fast-talking salespeople are outdated. Instead, he suggests that sales centers around the fundamental human activity of inspiring others. He suggests that, at its core, selling involves moving others to take action, a skill that is not limited to those with "sales" in their job titles. His research reveals that the skills traditionally associated with sales are now required across a variety of roles and industries.

Whether it's a teacher inspiring students to learn, a manager encouraging their team, or a customer service rep resolving a client's issue, these are all forms of motivating, influencing, *selling*. This principle is not only pivotal to our understanding of contemporary sales but also forms the bedrock of the IGNITE methodology.

The notion that "we're all in sales" can be daunting at first, but it's fundamentally about understanding the broader impact of our actions and communications. Consider how often you persuade someone in your daily life - convincing a colleague to support your project, negotiating with a vendor, or even influencing a friend's choice of restaurant. These are all forms of selling, rooted in building relationships and trust.

One of the key lessons from Pink's work is the shift in buyer behavior. Today's buyers are more informed and self-reliant, often completing a significant portion of their buying journey before even engaging with a salesperson. This means that the traditional sales pitch is no longer effective. Instead, sales professionals - and indeed, all employees - must focus on building relationships, creating value, and being genuinely helpful to potential buyers.

Moreover, Pink introduces the idea of "non-sales selling," which involves persuading, influencing, and convincing others without a direct financial transaction. This concept aligns perfectly with our approach to social selling. For example, when we share valuable content or engage in meaningful conversations online, we are practicing non-sales selling. These actions build credibility and relationships, which are foundational to successful social selling.

Social selling epitomizes the concept that everyone is in sales. It leverages social media platforms to build influence, make connections, grow relationships, and develop trust. These activities are not confined to the sales department; they are organizational responsibilities. Every employee can contribute to the company's social presence and reputation, thereby impacting sales.

This perspective isn't about diluting the specialized skills of sales professionals but rather recognizing that every touchpoint with a customer or prospect is an opportunity to influence and drive the sales process forward. This includes everything from customer service interactions to the messages put out by marketing to the content shared by the HR team.

The IGNITE methodology, which this book outlines, emphasizes the importance of social selling across all levels of an organization. By being approachable, sociable, and generous, employees can enhance their digital presence and engage more effectively with potential customers. This approach fosters a culture where everyone is empowered to contribute to the sales process, regardless of their formal role.

Moving forward, social media marketing will not center around "capital 'I' Influencers"

You know who I mean – those with hundreds of thousands, maybe even MILLIONS of followers. The ones who take the Main Stage at a convention and deliver the keynote address.

Social media won't even be about lower-case "i" micro-influencers (those with merely tens of thousands of followers). The ones who might deliver a workshop presentation or staff a booth at that same convention.

Sure, those will still be important. But not everybody can be a capital "I" influencer or even a lowercase "i" influencer. And that's OK. Not everybody wants to be a capital "I" Influencer.

But we can still find success through social media. Because relationships matter more now than ever before.

This is the Time of the Relator

In the DISC personality assessment tool a "Relator" typically refers to someone who values personal interaction and close relationships. They are often seen as warm, caring, and good at listening and maintaining deep, long-term relationships. Relators place a high value on personal connections and are often very supportive and nurturing in their interactions. They are typically empathetic and can understand and relate to the emotions of others. They tend to be excellent listeners, showing genuine interest in others' thoughts and feelings. And they generally prefer a collaborative approach – both internally and externally.

This is the Era of the Connector

In his book **The Tipping Point**, Malcolm Gladwell describes a similar personality type – Connectors. Connectors engage deeply with their network, forming close, personal bonds. Their interactions are often meaningful and impactful. Due to the depth of their relationships, Connectors are highly trusted and influential within their circle. Their recommendations and opinions are often valued and taken seriously. They prioritize maintaining a few strong relationships over having numerous acquaintances. They tend to invest a lot of time and effort in nurturing and maintaining their relationships.

People relate to people. People want to buy from people. But first, people want to connect with people.

What does this mean for you?

As a professor of Marketing, I tell my students -

Success in life is not simply about what you know.

But success in life is not just about who you know, either.

Success in life is about who knows you for what you know.

Your job, then, is to make sure more and more people know you for what you know.

What is the IGNITE Social Selling & Influence Sales Methodology?

IGNITE is the first social selling methodology built natively in the social media platforms. And while it is a stand-alone methodology, it can also be incorporated into an organization's existing practices, even aligning with other methodologies in place within the organization.

IGNITE is also the only social selling methodology independently verified and certified by a third party. Participants who complete the comprehensive IGNITE training program are eligible to apply and test for certification from the Institute for Sales Professionals (ISP).

IGNITE is a comprehensive social selling and influence program designed to be adaptable across various social media platforms. The principles and methodologies taught in IGNITE extend far beyond LinkedIn. In fact, IGNITE works best when used strategically across several social media platforms.

This program has been developed and deployed with organizations across the globe. From Fortune 500 organizations to solopreneurs, front-line sales representatives to CEOs, this program has spanned industries, job functions, time zones, and languages.

However, IGNITE is **_not_** -

A connect and pitch program - IGNITE is about building connection, and that isn't done by greeting a new connection with a *pitch-slap*.

You know the ones. They sound like a Carley Rae Jepsen song -

> *Hey!*
> *We just connected.*
> *And this is crazy!*
> *But here's my sale pitch.*
> *So buy some, maybe.*

Ummm... No. No thank you.

Additionally, IGNITE is **_not_** -

An overnight influencer program - IGNITE is about being active, growing your network, and contributing to the conversations taking place in your community. It is not about turning you into an "Influencer"; it's about leveraging your influence.

An AI automation tool - IGNITE is all about building personal connections. How can you do that through impersonal interaction? *"Have your bot call my bot and the can do lunch."*

And finally, IGNITE is **_not_** -

a LinkedIn training program.

This book is LinkedIn-centric, but the methodology is universal. The primary reason IGNITE starts with LinkedIn is that it is the largest professional platform where many business-to-business interactions occur. LinkedIn provides an excellent foundation for building a professional network, sharing industry-relevant content, and establishing thought leadership.

As the IGNITE methodology was being developed the ideal customer profiles of our clients and prospects (and their clients and prospects) were most often found on LinkedIn. However, the skills and strategies learned in IGNITE, and the essence of our 3 basic tenets, are applicable across multiple social media platforms, each with its own unique audience and style. While LinkedIn is a significant part of the training, the underlying strategies of social selling and influence are relevant and effective on other platforms like Twitter (now X), Facebook, Instagram, TikTok, and more.

The essence of IGNITE is to build genuine relationships, share valuable content, and engage with your audience authentically. These principles are not confined to any single platform. By understanding the unique dynamics of each social network, participants can effectively extend their reach and influence across the digital landscape.

This is about building a flywheel. People are getting to know you and your organization. The more of these channels that you're on, the more touchpoints you have and the more opportunities to meet people and strike up conversations with people. The goal is to create a cohesive and compelling presence that resonates with audiences wherever they are most active.

This Book is Divided Into 3 Sections

The book is divided into 3 sections, highlighted below. Like the chapters within, the book follows Simon Sinek's "Why – How – What" approach to messaging.

WHY: The State of The Industry For Sales and Marketing

Here you will gain insights into the evolving state of sales and marketing in the digital age. These chapters provide the foundational knowledge needed to navigate the current social-first landscape salespeople are struggling to navigate. By understanding the shift in the buyer's journey, you will be better equipped to engage with potential clients in a meaningful way, ultimately driving better sales outcomes.

HOW: The 3 Tenets Of IGNITE

Here you will learn about the core principles of the IGNITE methodology: **Be Approachable**, **Be Sociable**, and **Be Generous**. These tenets are essential for building a robust social enablement strategy and driving meaningful business outcomes. Each of these chapters provide actionable steps to enhance your social presence. By being approachable, sociable, and generous, you create a powerful online presence that not only attracts potential clients but also drives meaningful engagements and business success.

To support those who support Sales, this book includes icons with suggestions on how Leaders and various departments can enable Sales' efforts to **Be Approachable**, **Be Sociable**, and **Be Generous**.

 Leaders

 Enablement

 Marketing

 HR

WHAT: Social Enablement Action Steps

Here you will discover practical steps to implement the social enablement into your daily activities. You'll learn how to maintain consistency in your social media activities. You will also see how social enablement principles extend beyond Sales to other departments, and even work beyond an organizational environment.

Chapter Two

The Shift In The Buyer's Journey

How do you plan on reaching Buyers?

We often ask our prospects, "How do you reach (or plan on reaching) your buyers?"

Typical answers include -

- Cold Calling

- Email Marketing

- Advertising

Most established organizations apply some combination of the 3.

There are two problems with these approaches –

- Money, and

- Time

Phone, email, and advertising campaigns can be expensive to run, and these days they are taking longer and longer to show results - if they show results at all.

What if I told you money and time aren't even the biggest problem with these approaches?

The biggest problem with these approaches is that their effectiveness is diminishing. Significantly.

There was a time when you could send out an email blast and get an expected number of prospects to engage; you could make a certain number of cold calls and you could predict the number of conversations that would generate. You could run an ad and get an expected number of clicks.

In 2010 we heard from C-E-B, now a Gartner company, that the sales landscape was changing. According to their research, buyers were 57% down their buying journey before engaging with a salesperson. Buyers were more than half-way through their buying process. How is Sales supposed to influence the decision at that late stage?

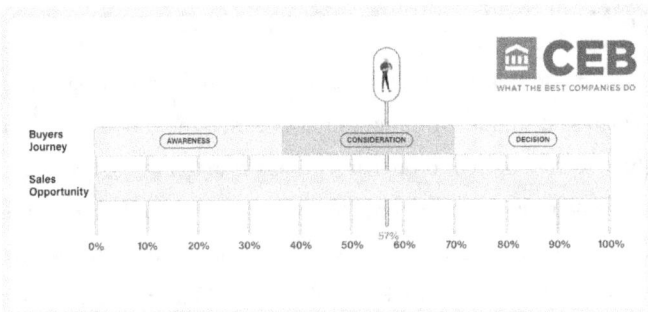

2010: Buyers are 57% through their buying journey before engaging with Sales.

But as I said, that statistic is over 10 years old.

The most recent data in this regard came out in January of 2024. In their **B2B Buyer Experience Report**, 6sense reports that buyers are now 70% through their journey and have already identified their likely choice of vendor before engaging with Sales. *Now what's a salesperson to do?*

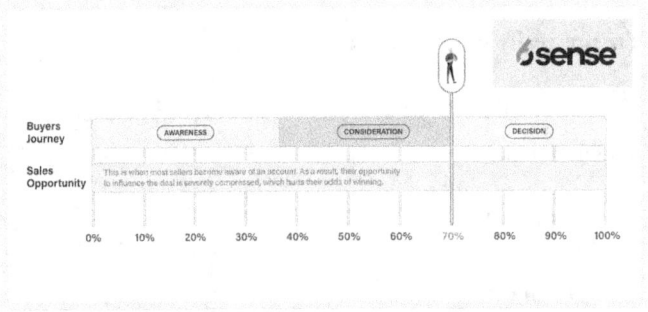

2024: Buyers are 70% through their buying journey and have identified their likely vendor of choice before engaging with Sales.

It gets even trickier!

Research also tells us that the number of people in buying teams has increased, and it continues to increase even more as budgets get tighter. Where it used to be that a project manager or a department head could make decisions for their organization's spending, now the CRO, the CFO, and the CEO want to be included in the buying process. We know that with every person who joins the buying team the likelihood of the deal closing is reduced, sometime dramatically.

And if that wasn't enough -

According to a recent Gartner report, "The desire for a seller-free buying experience has risen from 72% in 2022 to 75% in 2023."

In other words, *3 out of 4 people would rather go it alone than enlist the help of a salesperson.*

We're not really surprised at this, are we?

What do buyers think of salespeople? What does the general public say about salespeople?

- I don't like you.

- I don't trust you.

- I don't believe a word you say.

The reason this is important these days is because everything is ramping up.

Right now there's just over 8 billion people on the planet.

According to the **DIGITAL 2024 APRIL GLOBAL STATSHOT REPORT** by Simon Kemp, Founder of Kepios and Chief Data Analyst at DataReportal, 5.44 billion people - just over 67% of the world's population - are now on the internet.

5.07 billion people, that is 62.6% of the world's population, are considered active social media users. In other words - *nearly 2 out of every 3 people on the planet are considered active social media users.*

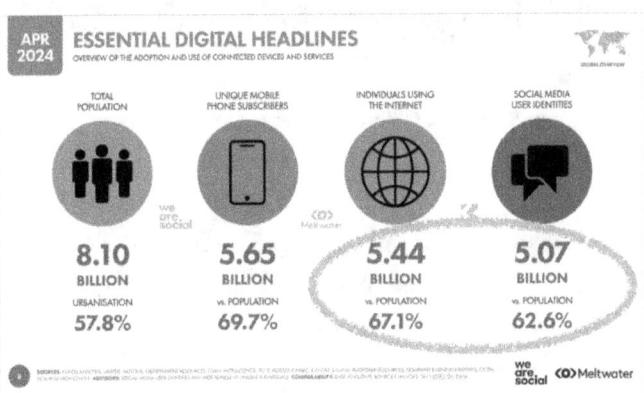

Credit: Simon Kemp, DataReportal

That's you, that's me, that's your prospects, your suppliers, your partners, your investors, your bankers... and that's your competition.

We've been following these statistics for a while, and every year we say, "It can't go up any higher." And every year it does. From that same report we see that the number of active users, as well as the percentage of the population who are considered active users, has not stopped growing.

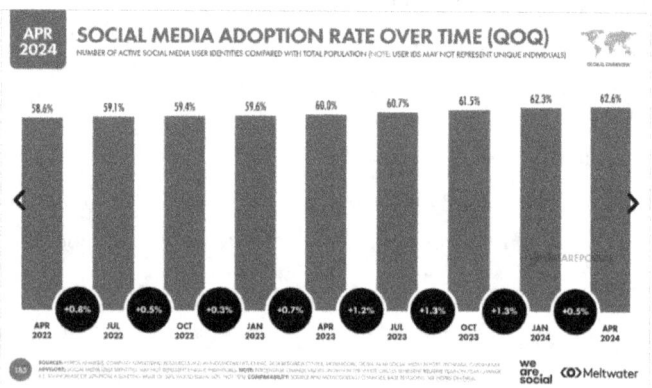

Credit: Simon Kemp, DataReportal

Everyone that we are connected to and everyone we need to be connected to are on social media. It's harder now to find someone who is beneficial to your business who is not on social media than it is to find those who are active there.

It's important that we understand this. It's important that we draw on this. Because what are they doing on social media? Besides posting family photos and keeping up with the latest fashion and lifestyle trends, they're learning, they're researching, they're seeking recommendations, and they are *searching*. Over 73% of social media users are using it to find out information about brands and products.

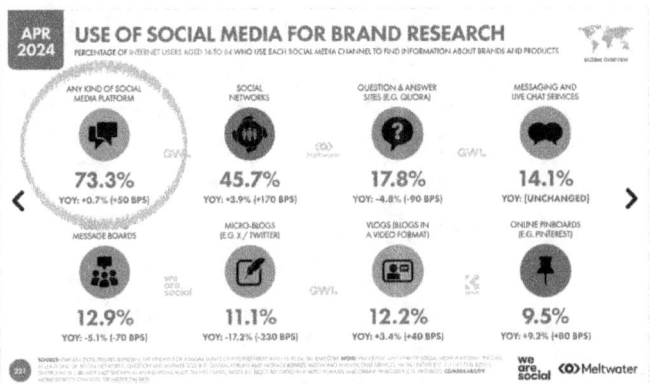

Credit: Simon Kemp, DataReportal

And whether or not you are present, whether or not you are approachable, whether or not you are sociable, and whether or not you are generous and helpful, they are using social media to find out about *and form opinions about **YOU**!*

If traditional sales and marketing tactics in this social-first world aren't working, what's left?

Let's talk about Social Selling.

Or as I like to call it, Social Enablement.

Because, as you will see, IGNITE is not about the traditional hard-sell, connect-and-pitch approach that so many quote/un-quote "social sellers" practice.

Not in any way.

Chapter Three

Understanding The IGNITE Methodology

How does your business use social media?

A question we often ask our audience.

Typical answers run the gamut, including -

- Old-school rule-makers saying, "Personal social media profiles are ___**not**___ for doing business!"

- "Marketing handles everything."

- "Some of us post on social media for business... sometimes."

- "We are actively using social media for business, always posting our latest offer."

Let's explore each of those.

"Personal social media profiles are _not_ for doing business!"

Maybe you believe personal social media profiles are not for doing business. I understand that sentiment.

But let me ask you -

- Are business conventions appropriate for doing business?

- Are networking events appropriate for doing business?

Of course they are.

What if you thought of LinkedIn not as the place you go to post your resume, but instead recognized it for what it is:

> LinkedIn is the largest, longest running, 24x7x365, virtual industry convention and networking platform that ever existed.

There's now over ONE BILLION people on the platform. And you not being an active participant is like going to a business convention or a networking event and talking to... *NOBODY.*

"Marketing handles everything."

Some believe they are maintaining an active social presence when they answer with, "Marketing handles everything," and they're content to re-share what Marketing puts out.

Maybe you leave social media up to your Marketing team. After all, social media is all about branding, right?

Let's take a closer look...

NIKE has about 8 ½ million Instagram followers. That's a pretty large audience, right? But who do you think might have a larger audience?

- Serena Williams has over *10 million followers*.

- LeBron James has almost **50 million followers**.

- And Cristiano Ronaldo has over ***90 million followers***.

How can that be? Why is it that NIKE spokespeople are more popular than NIKE itself? I mean, after all, they're all working for NIKE, right?

It's because people relate to people better than they relate to brands. And Marketing is all about branding. Yes, there is a place for branding, especially on social media, but branding - even personal branding - should not be your ONLY activity.

"Some of us post on social media for business... sometimes."

When people tell us this, they usually go on to say, "But we don't know what we get out of it," or, "We can't really tell if it's worth it."

Are you familiar with the flywheel effect? It's when small actions, repeated regularly, build on each other. And with each iteration you build up more and more momentum - more and more impact.

The same applies to social media. Random acts of being social results in random results – or more likely, no results at all. With social media, a regular, intentional cadence of activity will ultimately drive the results your business needs.

But what _are_ those activities? I can tell you this, it isn't a series of posts that say, **_"Buy my stuff!"_**

"We are actively using social media for business, always posting our latest offer."

To those who tell me they are always posting about their latest offer, I ask two follow-up questions: How is that working out? Is the phone ringing off the hook?

Of course not. Do you know why? Besides the fact that everyone likes to buy, but nobody likes to be sold to. **_It's because NOBODY sees it!_**

Your post is like a billboard in the middle of the desert. Nobody is driving by it, so nobody sees it. Well, not nobody. But not enough of the somebodys you want seeing it.

What is your plan for being seen by the people who you want to see you?

"All this sounds great."

By now others have said to me, "All this sounds great." But they have also later admitted to me that at this point they were sitting there sarcastically thinking, "What do we *do* on social media, share cat videos and sit around singing Kumbaya?"

No. We're here to do business.

Clients who are actively participating in our IGNITE 12-week training program - from leadership through to the front ranks - are seeing, on average

- A 30% increase in revenue AND

- Up to a 40% decrease in sales cycles. That is, deals are closing up to 40% faster.

Kumbaya indeed.

And as Steve Jobs was fond of saying...

"One More Thing"

According to HardNumbers.co.uk in their Coverage to Capital report exploring the link between thought leadership on social media and company valuations -

- Founders who are active on X (Twitter) receive, on average, 5% more in investment valuations

- Founders who are active on LinkedIn receive, on average, 20% more in investment valuations

By now you're probably asking,

What is Social Enablement?

Social Enablement is the process by which salespeople leverage social media to drive more conversations and ultimately drive more opportunity.

Social Enablement is also the process by which organizational Leaders, Enablement, Marketing, and HR professionals can support the Sales Team – *enable* them, as it were – in their social efforts.

What is IGNITE?

The IGNITE methodology is a comprehensive program designed to empower sales professionals and organizations to leverage social media platforms effectively. It provides both a strategic and tactical approach for individuals and organizations to leverage social media to drive more conversations and ultimately drive more opportunity. Unlike traditional sales methods, IGNITE focuses on enhancing visibility, building genuine relationships, and positioning sales teams as trusted advisors through a structured approach.

The Key Components of IGNITE

1. Ignite is made up of 3 Tenets:

- **Be Approachable:** Participants are led through the steps necessary to optimize digital profiles and manage personal branding to create positive first impressions.

- **Be Sociable:** Participants are guided through the process of actively engaging with and strategically growing their network through meaningful interactions and consistent content sharing.

- **Be Generous:** Participants are taught how to share valuable content and insights of others to establish their own reputation for thought leadership and fostering trust. Eventually they are trained how to develop their own meaningful content too.

2. IGNITE is about Digital Transformation:

IGNITE transcends typical sales training by facilitating a broader digital transformation within organizations. While the program typically starts with a Sales Team, because it emphasizes creating a social culture where employees across all departments contribute to the company's social presence and engagement it becomes a true organizational digital transformation program.

3. IGNITE Has Measurable Outcomes and a Clear ROI:

Sales Teams using the IGNITE methodology have reported significant improvements, including a 30% increase in revenue and a 40% reduction in the time required to close deals. This methodology has also helped in achieving higher employee engagement and retention, establishing trusted advisor status, and enhancing visibility in the marketplace.

4. IGNITE is a Comprehensive Training Program:

The IGNITE program involves a series of workshops, one-on-one coaching sessions, and continuous support to ensure participants effectively implement the strategies. This structured training is designed to produce predictable, repeatable results that go beyond generating pipeline and revenue, contributing to a stronger sense of purpose and belonging among employees.

How IGNITE Differs from Other Social Selling Programs

Unlike typical social selling programs, IGNITE is not limited to just using LinkedIn or just using X (Twitter). IGNITE provides a framework applicable across various social media platforms, adapting to the unique needs and goals of different organizations. In fact, IGNITE works best when its principles are applied *across* social media platforms. By focusing on consistent, strategic actions and the overall digital transformation of the organization, IGNITE aims to create a sustainable and impactful social organization.

In summary, IGNITE is a holistic approach to social selling that integrates personal branding, active networking, and content sharing into a cohesive strategy, driving both individual and organizational success in the digital age.

In fact, one could say that IGNITE is not about selling at all. IGNITE is about networking. IGNITE is about remembering the lessons Dale Carnegie taught us 85 years ago in his book **How to Win Friends and Influence People** and applying them in a prescriptive, strategic approach in today's social-first world.

IGNITE is a holistic approach to social selling that integrates personal branding, active networking, and content sharing into a cohesive strategy, driving both individual and organizational success in the digital age.

The Five Key Benefits of the IGNITE Methodology

The IGNITE methodology offers a transformative approach to social selling and influence, delivering substantial benefits across various aspects of an organization. Here's a narrative explaining the five key benefits of the IGNITE methodology: Visibility, Trusted Advisor Status, Pipeline Growth, Talent Acquisition, and Employee Engagement.

1. Visibility

In today's saturated digital landscape, standing out is more challenging than ever. Traditional marketing efforts often fall short, unable to break through the noise. The IGNITE methodology addresses this by empowering individuals and organizations to elevate their visibility through consistent and strategic social media engagement. By sharing valuable content and actively participating in relevant conversations, IGNITE participants enhance their personal and organizational brand recognition. This increased visibility not only attracts potential clients but also positions the organization prominently within its industry.

2. Trusted Advisor Status

Achieving trusted advisor status is crucial for building long-term relationships with clients and prospects. IGNITE helps individuals and organizations cultivate this status by focusing on authenticity, expertise, and consistent value delivery. By sharing insightful content and engaging in meaningful interactions, participants build credibility and trust. This approach moves beyond traditional selling, fostering a deeper connection where clients and prospects view the

IGNITE-trained professionals as reliable and knowledgeable advisors rather than mere vendors.

3. Pipeline Growth

As previously mentioned, one of the most tangible benefits of the IGNITE methodology is its impact on pipeline growth. By leveraging social media effectively, sales professionals can generate a steady stream of qualified leads. The methodology encourages proactive networking and consistent content sharing, which leads to increased engagement and more opportunities for conversations. These conversations are the seeds of new business, ultimately growing the sales pipeline and driving revenue. Organizations implementing IGNITE have reported up to a 30% increase in revenue and a 40% reduction in the time it takes to close deals.

4. Talent Acquisition

Attracting top talent is a significant challenge for many companies. IGNITE enhances an organization's employer brand by showcasing a dynamic, forward-thinking culture through social media. When employees actively share their professional journeys, insights, and company culture, it paints an attractive picture for potential recruits. This visibility makes the organization stand out as a desirable place to work, helping to attract the best talent in the industry.

5. Employee Engagement

Employee turnover is often a large cost to organizations - especially Sales Teams. After all, *empty seats don't fill quota*. Employee engagement is vital for a healthy, productive workplace. The IGNITE methodology fosters a sense of purpose and belonging among employees by involving them in the organization's social strategy. When employees feel their contributions are valued and that they are part of a larger mission, their engagement and job satisfaction increase. This shared sense of purpose not only enhances individual performance but also improves overall organizational cohesion and retention rates.

The IGNITE methodology transforms how organizations and individuals engage with the digital world. By enhancing visibility, establishing trusted advisor status, growing the pipeline, attracting top talent, and boosting employee engagement, IGNITE provides a comprehensive framework for sustainable success in the modern business environment. This methodology is not just about social selling; it's about creating a socially enabled, digital-first organization ready to thrive in today's interconnected landscape.

Chapter Four

Be Approachable

Why: Controlling Your Digital Narrative

I magine you were finishing up a business trip and needing to head to the airport quickly to catch your flight home. It's a beautiful crisp spring day. The roads are dry. Conditions are fine, but you have an hour to get there and it's about 30 highway miles away. You must get to the airport quickly to make your flight.

Here we see images of two cars. One is an antique Model-T Ford, the other is a sleek new sportscar. Which car would choose?

For a sightseeing drive there really is no wrong answer. You may have looked at the two choices and said that antique car looks like it would be great fun to ride in. Or maybe the sleek and sporty model is more your style.

But in this situation, you're in a bit of a rush to get to the airport and you need to drive on the highway to get there. Obviously, you would look at the two and pick the sporty model.

The fact is, either one could be nothing more than a cardboard cut-out or a model car for a movie, but it has no engine in it. We needed to look at our options, decide quickly, and go. In this situation we look at our choices and pick the one that will (seemingly) obviously get us to the airport on time; we choose the sports car.

We ALL jump to conclusions

The fact is we ALL jump to conclusions by what we see. And we are all impacted by the conclusions others make of us by what they see of us, and our online presence is no exception. When we are present on social media, we are open to judgment; we are at the whim of the conclusions others make when they see our social presence.

Our job, then, is to make people jump to the conclusions that we want them to jump to. We *can* make them jump to the conclusions that we want them to jump to if we are intentional about how we present ourselves and what we do when we are online.

Did you know?

According to LinkedIn, they have now reached one billion users as of November 2023. On that platform you will find:

- 1.7 million Heads of Communication

- 8.2 million with the title CEO

- 8.5+ million Sales Directors

- *20+ million Business Development Managers*

Why does this matter? On LinkedIn they all look alike. They all sound alike!

They're all the #1 choice, top performing in their industry. They are passionate about their role and they all put their clients first. And they all look and sound like the millions of their peers in similar roles in similar industries.

It's the Gestalt Theory in action

The Gestalt theory says that humans perceive the world in large part based on their previous experiences. We mix and match previous experiences to develop a quick perception of new encounters, like when we jump to conclusions about movie set cars and assume they can drive us to the airport. The more something new resembles something known to us, the less it stands out as new or different.

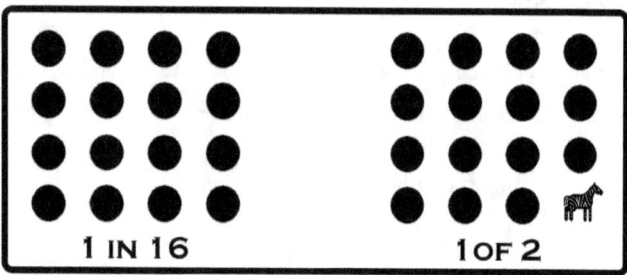

Let's use smaller numbers to paint the picture. On the left we see a group of 16 individuals all represented similarly; in this case each is represented as a circle in a 4 by 4 grid of circles. In fact, one may ask: is it really a group of 16 individuals, or is it *one* group that has 16 look-alike members?

Contrast that with the second group of 16 on the right. There we have 15 circles and one zebra. It's clear that one stands out. In this group of 16 it could be argued that you actually have two distinctly different groups – one group of 15 look-alikes and one group of one - a unique member in a group unto themselves. In this context the zebra goes from being considered one of 16 (circles) to one of 2 (circles and non-circles - zebras in fact, of which, they are the only one).

We use this same approach in developing your social media profile.

> **Go from looking like one of millions to**
> ***one-in-a-billion*****!**

"But I don't want to stand out."

"But I don't want to stand out," you say. "I want to conform."

Great news. You're doing that now. How's that working out for you?

Standing out doesn't have to be absurd or extreme.

When my children were young, sometimes they'd get bored, and they'd act up. I would ask them, "I know you're looking for attention, but do you want *good attention*, or do you want *bad attention*?"

Standing out for the sake of standing out is not necessarily going to drive good attention. But we're here to guide you through this. Let's drive more good attention.

 Leaders can enable their sales representatives by -

- Setting the expectation that an active social media presence is acceptable - *and expected*.

- Being clear about the "rules". (When it comes to someone's personal social media profile, organizations should be wary of too many rules, but clear guidelines from the onset are helpful.)

- Modeling the behavior

How: Shaping Perceptions

Shaping perceptions on social media is all about ensuring that the impression people form of you aligns with the image you want to project. This process involves two key elements: your passive social presence and your active social behavior. By strategically managing both your passive and active social presence, you can effectively shape how others perceive you, ensuring they see you as the knowledgeable and valuable professional you are.

Passive Social Presence

Your passive social presence includes everything that people can learn about you without any real-time interaction. This primarily means your profile. An optimized profile works for you even when you're not online. It should communicate your expertise and value proposition clearly and effectively.

For example, an optimized social media profile might include:

- A compelling headline that draws people closer to you.

- A professional photo and banner that visually conveys you, not just your employer or your brand.

- A detailed and engaging "About" section that tells your story, highlighting your unique skills and experiences. But most importantly, it should tell us about the why behind your story.

- On LinkedIn your experiences section should help people learn more about you, your accomplishments, and your motivations - not simply the tasks you performed or the value proposition of your previous employer.

- A strong profile isn't simply an electronic version of your resume or CV; it's a tool for shaping how others perceive you, making sure they jump to the conclusions you want them to.

Active Social Presence

Your active social presence includes all the actions you take on social media - comments, likes, shares, as well as the content you create like posts, blogs, and videos. While your passive presence works in the background, your active behavior should consistently drive people back to your well-crafted profile. It's about reinforcing the message your profile sends, maintaining visibility, and engaging with your network in meaningful ways.

For example, an effective active social presence might include:

- Engaging with others by liking, commenting, and sharing posts from your connections. This serves to help to build relationships and increases your visibility.

- Participating in discussions related to your industry, providing thoughtful input. This helps you to stay top-of-mind within your professional community.

- Regularly posting, sharing insightful and relevant content that reflects your expertise and interests. This keeps your network informed and again increases your visibility.

- Creating original content - blogs, articles, videos, etc. - that showcase your knowledge and add value to your network and to your industry. This positions you as someone in your field worth being connected to - even a thought leader.

Your active social presence should consistently reinforce the message your profile sends, maintaining your visibility and engaging with your network in meaningful ways. Just like your profile, your interactions on social media should be strategic, authentic, and aligned with your professional goals.

 Enablement can offer training on building and maintaining a professional and engaging social presence.

What: Crafting an Engaging Social Presence

All the active things we do online are designed to drive people to our profiles to learn more about us. **Be Approachable** is about crafting an engaging passive social presence. We will address your active social presence in **Be Sociable** and **Be Generous**.

Something important to note: For some there is a serious concern about attracting the wrong kind of attention from the wrong kind of people. This is completely understandable. Of course, how you present yourself and how much you share is up to you. But if you are leveraging your social profile to get closer to people, it helps to let them get closer to you - to the extent that is comfortable for you.

It should also be noted that social media platforms are constantly testing, changing, and developing new features. And new platforms always seem to be popping up. While it's important to understand and keep up with these changes, some of the most important aspects of any social media profile remain constant and universal across platforms. The way people see you on one platform should be aligned with the way they see you across all of them. To do otherwise is likely to send mixed messages. People won't try to work out the confusion - they'll simply move on to the next person.

We're going to address some of the most important elements of your social profile here, but not all of them. Simply because it's not discussed here does not mean it can be ignored. Elements like usernames, custom URLs, pinned items, recommendations (both received and given), and other sections of your social media profiles all serve to provide a comprehensive picture of you. Keep in mind that the more thorough your profile, and the more you use it to draw *good attention*, the more you stand out like a unicorn.

 Annual reviews provide a great opportunity for Leaders to recognize their employees with a LinkedIn recommendation.

Your Headline/ Bio

At the time of this printing your LinkedIn headline can include up to 220 characters. However, it should be noted that only approximately 55-65 show every time you leave a comment or create a post – so let's make them count. On X (formerly Twitter) your bio can include up to 160 characters. But just because X calls the field "bio", who says it has to be your bio? I mean, who could possibly truncate their life into 160 characters? (For reference, Instagram's bio limits users to 150 characters, Facebook 101, and TikTok 80.)

We want to lean into the Gestalt theory and use this space to drive good attention. At the end of this chapter you will see an exercise designed to help you revise your headline into something that takes you from looking like one of millions into ***one-in-a-billion***.

Professional Imagery

Is your current background blank or the default stock image? Use this space to share a little insight into you – share a favorite vacation spot or a hobby. Maybe make a collage of a few of the things you want us to know about you. Show us something different from what every other social media profile is showing.

 Marketing can contribute to social enablement by creating graphic templates tailored to each platform's dimensions.

Your profile picture should show you. Just you. And it should be just your head and shoulders; wider shots become harder to recognize as the profile pictures are displayed in-line with posts and comments. Use a professional-looking headshot that is consistent across all your social platforms. Some say black and white photos are more professional, others advocate for the use of color; whichever you choose is up to you, but even that choice is telling us something about you and how you want us to perceive you.

 HR can support new hires by taking not just an ID photo but a true headshot suitable for all their social profiles.

Your About Section

Unique to LinkedIn, at this time you have approximately 2,600 characters in your About section to let us know about you - you as a human, you as a person not just as a job title, you as someone who's done interesting stuff in your life.

This is where you make a connection with the reader. You want them to read your profile and say, "I want to know more about this person. I want to connect with them." All technical info and qualifications are not going to capture the attention of your readers. Being relatable will.

LinkedIn recently announced that In March (2024) they will be moving the About section to the top of your profile. According to LinkedIn, this is "so that people can easily grasp your professional story." LinkedIn is confirming they want you to tell your story. Don't let anyone dissuade you otherwise.

Your Experience Section

Another profile element unique to LinkedIn is the Experience section. This is *not* a resume or CV. Alternatively, a lot of people advertise for their employers and past employers in this valuable real estate. "I worked at XYZ Corporation. XYZ manufactures..."

But look at the title of that section - it's called "Experience". LinkedIn wants you to share your experience in that role, not boring corporate-speak or an advertisement for someone else. There's now 2,000 words available for each experience, so why give me just 10?

Use as many of those 2,000 words as you can to tell me:

1. Why you took that job

2. The wins and the challenges you had while there

3. The lessons learned from that experience, and

4. Why you left

Unlike with a resume where brevity is expected, even necessary, use all 2,000 words as an opportunity to tell your story, to allow me to get closer to you. And don't simply use bullets or sentence fragments; use a conversational format and tone. In 2,000 words, share with us all four of the answers to those questions. And to be clear, you should do that with 2,000 words for each experience.

"Why should I use 2,000 words to tell you about my job?"

You're not telling me about your job - you're telling me about you! You are giving me an opportunity to get closer to you. And it's not about the 2,000 words; it's about keeping the reader's attention. For every minute they spend reading about you, that's one less minute they have to read your competitor's profile.

This is also an opportunity to ensure your profile is filled with the right keywords. LinkedIn search is not limited to your headline. Search results are gathered based on the contents of your entire profile. Take advantage of this; use the space in your Experience as an opportunity to showcase your role in the context of the terms people in your industry search for - the keywords.

(Search results are also dependent upon your proximity to the person searching - i.e. geography and 1st connection, 2nd connection, etc. - which is why our next section, **Be Sociable**, becomes so important.)

Be Approachable: Final Thoughts

Building a strong passive and active social presence is just the beginning. By carefully crafting how we present ourselves online, we ensure that others jump to the conclusions we want them to, positioning ourselves as knowledgeable and valuable professionals. However, being approachable is not the end goal; it's the foundation.

As we move forward, we'll learn about the next crucial tenet: **Be Sociable**. Here, we'll explore the art of networking in the digital age. It's not just about making connections, but about engaging authentically and meaningfully with your network. We'll discuss strategies to nurture these connections, share engaging content, and expand your influence.

After understanding how to be approachable and how to be sociable, we'll transition to the final tenet: **Be Generous**. This is where we'll focus on the power of content creation and thought leadership. By sharing valuable insights and resources, you'll reinforce your expertise and foster deeper relationships with your network.

Together, these three tenets - **Be Approachable**, **Be Sociable**, and **Be Generous** - form the core of the IGNITE methodology. They work in tandem to create a robust social selling strategy that not only helps you build a powerful online presence but also drives meaningful business outcomes.

EXERCISE: MadLibs Headline

Here's an exercise designed to help you with changing your headline. We'll apply Gestalt thinking to drive *good attention*.

But first, a disclaimer

Here you may find things that will take you outside of your comfort zone. And some of the things may be completely counter to what quote/ unquote "gurus" have taught you. That's fine. Take what you want from this and leave the rest behind. But you came here because what you have been doing up to this point has not been driving the results you hoped for; this is a chance to change that. Also, if you see yourself in some of these things and don't like how they are portrayed them, please know that no insult is intended. This exercise is intended to drive *good attention*. If something is being called out it's because either it's not necessarily driving *good attention*, or worse, it's not driving attention at all.

The first thing most people see when they encounter you on LinkedIn is your headline. Not only is it at the top of your profile, at least a part of it shows on each and every post and comment you make.

By default, your LinkedIn headline is set to your "Current Job Title" at your current "Employer".

Write those down:

Current job title _____ at **Current employer**

._____ at _____.

For me that would read <u>Founder at Flywheel Results LLC</u>

Impressive, right? Maybe not. The only people "impressed" are those who scour LinkedIn searching for Founders so they can pitch their own stuff.

And this headline is certainly not something I would consider approachable. It doesn't really help people get to know me; more to the point, it doesn't really help them get *closer* to me.

Ego? Check. Helpful? No, not really. By the way, there are over 9.6 ***MILLION*** *people on LinkedIn with the word "Founder" in their job title. So it's not particularly unique either.*

Your LinkedIn headline can include up to 220 characters. However, it should be noted that only approximately 55-65 show when you create a post or leave a comment – ***so let's make them count***.

On Twitter (now X) your bio can include up to 160 characters. But just because X calls the field "bio", who says it ***has to be*** your bio? I mean, who could possibly truncate their life into 160 characters???

That's daunting. Let's see if we can find a way to make this process easier. Did you ever play Madlibs as a kid? We're going to apply the Madlib approach to our headline and bio to come up with some creative ways of generating ***good attention***.

The Quote Headline

Here's a simple one. Think of a quote from your favorite book or movie and write it down:

Favorite quote by **Source**:

. _____ .

. _____ .

Here's one I like from Mark Twain:

<u>"It is better to keep your mouth closed and let people think you are a fool than to open it and remove all doubt." -Mark Twain</u>

What do you think? I'd say it's fine. There's certainly nothing wrong with it. It's not particularly **_unique_**, but I don't expect _a lot_ of people to use it for their profile headline. I guess my problem with it is it's not **_personal_** enough. It doesn't bring people _closer_.

The Pipe Headline

What do you think of the pipe line headlines? You know the ones. The ones where they try to list everything they do in their headline so they separate each thing they do with a long vertical line – _that's called a pipe_. They're very busy as a <u>Keynote Speaker | Author | Life Coach | Dog Mom</u>.

This is definitely **_personal_**. But is it **_unique_** if so many others are doing it? I checked. There are thousands of "dog moms", "girls dads", etc.

What about the exes? You know, "Ex-Facebook, Ex-Amazon, Ex-Google"? Again, not particularly unique, but it also leaves me wondering – What makes you incapable of staying on with any one of these stellar companies?

It also makes me think of NFL pro football players. At the beginning of the game when the broadcast shows a player introducing themselves it usually includes a brief video of them saying their name, their position, and where they went to college. Some players are having fun with it now. Instead of saying their college, they'll list their elementary school or middle school. We can have fun with that too.

Write down your alma maters, your Grammar School, your Middle School, and your High School:

._____|_____|_____.

For me that would look like:

Ex-Hoover School | Ex-Melrose Veterans Memorial Middle School | Ex-Melrose High School

Definitely unique, well except for the 250 people who graduated with me, about 50 who were with me since Hoover School.

But is it **approachable**? Only some are likely to get the NFL reference. To them, I become *completely approachable!* Unfortunately, to most it's an obscure take and may not be very approachable.

The Superlative Headline

You know what everybody loves even more than a superstar athlete? A relatable one. What if we lean into our lack of athletic prowess with a little bit of self-depreciating humor? Let's show the world just how good we are at a commonplace activity.

Think of an everyman's sport, something you definitely would not find at the Olympics. Maybe it was a popular pastime on the school playground from your childhood; maybe it's a game that never existed except in a fiction novel. Alternatively, list an everyday hobby or activity, something that nobody would typically take pride in excelling at.

Now imagine a universe where being highly skilled at the mundane is suddenly considered extraordinary. What would be considered a high level of achievement? Maybe it's playing for a college or pro team. Maybe it's being showcased in the museum or hall of fame for this skill.

Write down your "skill" and where it's showcased:

Superlative skill at **Where it's showcased**:

_____

Some examples might be:

Outstanding kickball player. Could have started for Notre Dame.

I love a good game of Poohsticks - I could have gone pro

My childhood artwork is proudly displayed in the museum known as my mother's kitchen[*]

* The best part of this one is that the first 55 characters, the part that will always display, ends at "museum".

The Meme Headline

A popular meme formats is based on "What people think I do." We can leverage this humorous and often revealing glimpse into the disconnect between perception and reality.

How do different people view what you do? It could be simple, like your job title, or something exaggerated - even something completely off base. Is there a common misunderstanding of what your role entails? Lean into that!

How does your family, especially your mother, understand your profession? And most importantly, how does that contrast with what you actually do? The more simplistic or humorous take, reflecting the loving but sometimes clueless view of a parent or loved-one, the better.

What do you really do: This is the core of your role, boiled down to its most truthful essence. Alternatively, if there's a common inside joke known by those in your industry (IYKYK), use it!

Here's are some examples:

CEO

People think I make all the big decisions. My mother thinks I own the company. Really, I attend endless meetings and play email dodgeball.

People think I'm always closing deals. My mother thinks I'm a millionaire. Really, I manage chaos and wonder what happened to my work-life balance.

Sales Leader

People think I just push for higher numbers. My mother thinks I'm the office cheerleader. Really, I herd cats and put out fires daily.

People think I make all the big decisions. My mother thinks I attend meetings all day. Really, I play referee between sales and marketing.

Salesperson

People think I'm a smooth talker. My mother thinks I chat with people all day. Really, I perfect the art of rejection and survive on coffee.

People think I close deals with ease. My mother thinks I give away free stuff. Really, I talk to voicemail and get ghosted by prospects.

Enablement

People think I'm the Director of Sales Enablement. Mom thinks I sell stuff. Really, I fix broken things.

People think I just schedule training. Mom thinks I'm a motivational speaker. Really, I bribe reps with swag and remind them to use the CRM.

Marketer

People think I make flashy ads. My mother thinks I work in TV. Really, I obsess over hashtags and argue with designers.

People think I just post on social media. My mother thinks I'm in PR. Really, I stalk competitors and survive on likes and shares.

HR Specialist

People think I just hire and fire people. My mother thinks I'm a counselor. Really, I decode benefits packages and host awkward team-building events.

People think I handle complaints all day. My mother thinks I'm the office therapist. Really, I attend endless meetings and play phone tag with recruiters.

Now you try

What people think I do:

._____.

What my mother thinks I do:

._____.

What I really do:

._____.

Don't Forget: Once you have figured out your headline for LinkedIn, you need to map this over to your X bio and across all your other social platforms.

Is my headline good?

Some people are hesitant to try this, not wanting to get it wrong. There is no "wrong" answer, but there are two questions you can ask to measure whether or not your new headline is working for you:

Is it driving *good* attention?

Does it help people get closer to you?

Sometimes you have to try something out to know whether or not it's right for you. The great part about this exercise is that not only is it easy to change your headline, it's recommended that you do so regularly.

Chapter Five

Be Sociable

Why: Business Has Not Changed

The second tenet of IGNITE is **Be Sociable**. It's about leveraging social media platforms to build your network *intentionally*.

I know. I know. Networking. **YUCK!** Right? So many people say, "I hate networking!"

I get it. I too cringe at the thought of putting myself out there - *I'm an introvert*. I hate the thought of nepotism. And I can't stand the thought of the good ole' boys' network!

You heard me say this before:

Success in life is not simply about what you know.

But success in life is not just about who you know, either.

Success in life is about who knows you for what you know.

Your job, then, is to make sure more and more people know you for what you know.

Think of it this way:

If you're lucky, in your Rolodex - be it physical, digital, or mental - you have:

-A good doctor,

-A sharp lawyer, and

-A trustworthy mechanic.

If you are really lucky, you also have a plumber and an electrician who will return your calls.

But when people think of the solution you provide, who has you in **their** Rolodex?

Networking has always been a cornerstone of professional success, serving as the backbone for building relationships, exchanging ideas, and opening doors to new opportunities. Traditionally, networking relied heavily on face-to-face interactions, which allowed individuals to create personal connections through physical presence and direct communication.

However, with the advent of digital technology, networking has undergone a significant transformation. Today, social media platforms serve as the one of the primary places where digital networks gather. In the process these platforms offer a new paradigm that expands the reach, efficiency, and impact of networking activities.

Digital networking removes the constraints of geography and time, making it accessible to anyone with an internet connection. This convenience allows professionals to grow and maintain their networks more efficiently, without the need for constant travel.

The COVID-19 pandemic forced a sudden and drastic transformation in how business was conducted, particularly affecting "road warriors" who relied heavily on travel for face-to-face meetings and networking. With travel restrictions in place, many professionals had to quickly adapt to digital-first interactions. Virtual meetings, online conferences, and digital networking became the norm.

Even though travel has largely resumed, because of its ease of use, scalability, and lower costs, the preference for digital-first business has remained. Professionals have found that digital networking is not only more convenient but also highly effective, allowing them to maintain and grow their networks - and thereby grow their business - without the need for constant travel.

Additional benefits include -

Cost-Effectiveness: Digital networking significantly reduces the costs associated with traditional networking methods. In addition to eliminating the need for travel expenses, individuals and businesses can reduce or eliminate costs associated with venue rentals, printed materials, or other logistical costs related to attending in-person events.

Scalability: The ability to connect with numerous people simultaneously is a hallmark of digital networking. This scalability provides more opportunities to connect to and engage with a broader audience and build a more extensive network than traditional methods allow.

Data and Analytics: Real-time feedback on engagement enables professionals to refine their strategies and focus on what works best. The use of analytics tools helps in making informed decisions, enhancing the effectiveness of networking efforts.

Enhanced Visibility: As highlighted in our previous chapter, **Be Approachable**, a well-maintained online presence ensures continuous visibility, even when offline, which is a significant advantage over traditional in-person networking practices. Through active engagement (as we'll explain here in **Be Sociable**), and content sharing (discussed in the next chapter, **Be Generous**), professionals can achieve greater visibility in their field. In other words, more and more people will know you for what you know.

We're going to use all this to our advantage.

How well connected are you?

Before we talk about growing your network, let's take a temperature check. Take a moment to look at the size of your network right now. But please note, this will be not about adding connections simply for the sake of adding connections.

There's quite a big distinction between the size of your network and the number of your connections. Maybe you've already got a thousand, two thousand, five thousand or more connections on LinkedIn. The problem is you don't know who most of them are. Truthfully, most of them don't know who you are either.

Having a lot of connections is not the same as having a big network. A big network is having a lot of people who do know who you are. We're going to work on that.

This isn't a competition, either. It does not matter whether you have more, fewer, or the same number of connections as everyone else. (Inevitably, there will *always* be someone with more - and that's ok.) This is a matter of measuring you against you. Understanding where you are at the start of an endeavor can provide you with a good idea of where you are going along the way.

How: Shifting a Legacy Network to a Desired Network

For most of us, our network, like our Rolodex, is made up of friends, family, and the numerous connections to former colleagues we have built over our careers. These connections often form clusters based on the various roles and industries we have worked in. For many professionals, especially those who have transitioned into different roles across various industries or fields, their networks are composed of an eclectic collection of people from a vast number of varied backgrounds.

While this is a great depiction of where we've been, does this reflect where we want to go? We need to ask ourselves a critical question: Is our network in the right place? For many, the answer is no.

But simply having a large network is not inherently valuable. The true value lies in having connections that can drive your current objectives. Even those with large networks sometimes find little value in them. If your goal is to have conversations with sales leaders, having 10,000 connections in legal services or human resources might not provide an immediate opportunity to start these conversations.

Yes, you should continue to work on maintaining relationships with your existing network - your Legacy Network - but if you want to get in front of people in roles or industries vastly different from those to whom you are already connected, there is still a lot work to be done. It's essential to ensure that your network connections align with your current goals.

This doesn't mean limiting your network to people with specific job titles; it's about connecting with several of the people who are a part of the organizations and industries you are working with - or hope to work with - today.

Your Dunbar Network

The Dunbar Number, named after anthropologist Robin Dunbar, is a fascinating concept. It's essentially a cognitive limit, estimated at around 150, that represents the maximum number of meaningful social connections a person can effectively maintain. Beyond this number, our ability to nurture and engage with relationships tends to diminish, leading to missed opportunities and untapped potential.

Like the rings on a bullseye, some in your network are closer to you than others. The more or less frequently you engage with certain people, the more or less likely they are to be considered a part of an inner ring. And this is an ever-changing set of rings, an ever-changing group of 150, as relationships ebb and flow.

You may be content with the number of LinkedIn connections you have. And no doubt the quality is there. It's likely to be made up predominantly of family and friends, and they will always be part of your inner circle - the core, never-changing part of your 150.

But what if there was a way to optimize this natural limit? Enter the **Dunbar Network**. This is the term I'm using to describe a strategic approach to cultivating and nurturing your most valuable connections.

It Starts with Connecting Intentionally

Imagine if there were two organizations each with over 30,000 employees, each in the same industry, and you wanted to sell to both. With traditional methods of outreach (cold calling, cold emailing, and advertising) you will have varying degrees of success, but more or less the same level of success with each. (Which is to say, not much.)

You might look at the first company and find that you have zero connections there. Any outreach to them would be entirely cold. But with the second company you have over 500 connections. You're not necessarily looking to sell to any one of those individuals. But you can leverage those connections to significantly elevate your chances of reaching your ideal target audience within the organization.

Even if none of those 500 connections are part of the buying team, having a broad network within the organization increases the likelihood that some of your connections are connected to the people you need to reach. Through the relationships you've built, you might find a pathway to connect with the right team.

But even without a direct introduction, your active presence on social media, coupled with your contributions to industry thought leadership, increases the chances of serendipity. As much as 50% of the content we see in our newsfeed is created by our second connections, based on the reactions to it by our first connections.

As you share content worth engaging with, this improves the chances that your content flows through the feeds of your connections and potentially reaches your connections' colleagues on the buying team. This approach helps you become a recognized name, making it more likely that you'll be remembered and considered when an opportunity arises.

By being connected to many within the organization and consistently sharing valuable, engaging content - ***not just sales pitches*** - you increase the odds that your insights will resonate and help you get on the radar of those you would like to speak to.

The more connections you have within an organization, and the more relevant and engaging the content you put out (more on this later), the better your chances of being noticed by the right people. This strategic approach to networking is about building relationships and sharing value, ensuring you're seen as a thought leader and a valuable connection, rather than just another salesperson.

Let me be clear: This is not about connecting and pitching!

This is about connecting and **_connecting_** – that is, establishing an online connection first, then subsequently establishing a true connection. And as discussed already, none of the people I connect to might be the person or team I need to sell to, but by connecting with more people intentionally I am significantly elevating the chances that at least some of them will be connected to my ideal target audience.

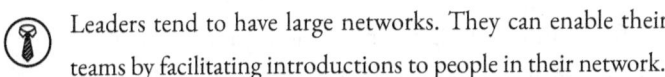 Leaders tend to have large networks. They can enable their teams by facilitating introductions to people in their network.

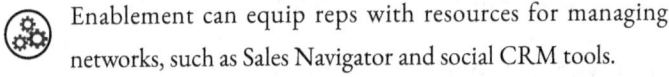 Enablement can equip reps with resources for managing networks, such as Sales Navigator and social CRM tools.

HR can enable the entire organization by making connecting with coworkers part of the onboarding experience.

Simply Growing a Network is Not Enough

We all have people in our network that have connected to us and then we've never seen nor heard from them again. They've never had a conversation with us, they've never published anything, in fact, they've never done anything online to remind us that they exist. We need to make sure that's not how we're perceived.

Depth of connection is also crucial. Simply being connected to someone doesn't mean much. Would buy from someone just because you follow each other on X? Probably not. Would you hire someone just because they're a connection on LinkedIn? With no other engagement - no.

Do you know your connections well? More importantly, do they know you and see you as a valuable addition to their network? Do they understand and value what you bring to the table? Do they know you for what you want to be known for? It's vital to continually reinforce that you're a good person to know and have in their network. It's crucial to ensure that your network includes people who recognize your value and can mobilize support for you when needed.

Crafting authentic digital interactions means creating genuine connections through meaningful engagement. For a network to be meaningful we need to be active within that network. How?

Quality Over Quantity

While it's tempting to be present on every platform, it's more strategic to focus on a few where you can be genuinely active. A meaningful presence on a few platforms is far more valuable than a superficial presence on many. It's about ensuring that your interactions on these platforms are authentic and valuable.

Authentic Engagement with Comments and Likes

Being responsive is at the heart of genuine digital engagement. It's not enough to merely have a profile; you must actively participate and interact with your audience. The beauty of the digital space is that you can interact with lots of people across geographies and industries without the constraints of time and travel. Responding to your connections' posts, messages, comments, and engagement shows that you value and acknowledge your relationships. This responsiveness fosters trust and builds stronger ties.

Consistency

Consistency in your interactions and content is key. Regular engagement helps in maintaining visibility and staying top-of-mind within your network. Whether it's posting content or engaging with others, ensure that your presence is steady and reliable.

Transparency and Honesty

Being transparent and honest in your interactions builds credibility. Share your successes as well as your challenges. People appreciate authenticity, and showing your human side can make you more relatable and trustworthy.

Personalized Interactions

When interacting online, personalize your responses. Address people by their names, refer to specific points they have made, and add your personal touch to the conversation. This level of personalization shows that you are genuinely engaged and interested in what they have to say.

Active Listening

Engage in active listening. Pay attention to what others are saying, ask follow-up questions, and show empathy. This not only makes your interactions more meaningful but also helps you understand your audience better.

Building Relationships

Networking is not just about expanding your connections list but about deepening relationships. Engage in conversations that go beyond surface-level interactions. Ask questions, provide thoughtful feedback, and be genuinely interested in your connections' updates and achievements. As public conversations turn to personal interactions, invite people to have a one-on-one call.

Blending Physical and Digital Interactions

Attending industry conventions, networking events, and conferences are still common business practices. Leverage the power of social media to improve your chances of having meaningful conversations there. Connect with registered attendees in advance on the social platform(s) where they are most active. Use these exchanges to schedule 15-minute meet ups during the event (most events now use apps to help with this). And follow-up after the event offering to exchange notes.

Leaders are often asked to speak at events. They can enable their teams by bringing some along, or forgo an appearance and suggest someone from your team instead.

Marketing can enable sales reps by recommending them for speaking opportunities at events they are sponsoring. Alternatively, showcase sales reps at events created and hosted by Marketing.

HR can enable sales reps by ensuring they have the flexibility and time to engage in networking events and activities without compromising their work-life balance.

Engaging Content

Sharing valuable content that resonates with your audience is essential. This content should not only reflect your expertise but also be relevant and engaging. Regularly sharing industry-related insights and personal stories helps in building a narrative that others can connect with.

Enablement can help sales reps integrate your organization's sales processes into the content they share. Encourage them to share content aimed at supporting the various stages, from awareness to decision making - and beyond.

(We'll talk more about sharing and creating content in the next chapter, **Be Generous**.)

Crafting authentic digital interactions is about more than just being active online. It's about being present, engaging genuinely, and building meaningful relationships. By focusing on responsiveness, quality content, personalized interactions, and consistent engagement, you can create a digital presence that is both authentic and impactful. This approach not only enhances your personal brand but also fosters a network of connections that are truly valuable and supportive.

What: Building and Nurturing a Robust Dunbar Network

If success is determined by who knows you for what you know, and your job is to make sure more and more people know you for what you know, success then comes from continually building your network.

What do we need to do to grow our network intentionally?

The key thing is to connect. A lot. We need to be making sure that we're constantly growing our network and growing it in a very focused way. We need to be in front of the people that we want to be in front of, noticed by the companies we want to be noticed by, and seen by the people that have shown through their actions that they are predisposed to engaging with us.

It's important to note that connecting to people is not the same as building a network. It's not just about getting these people in your network; it's about making sure that they know you for what you know. A connection is just the start of the process, not the end-goal.

We've got two things that we can do to grow our network –

- Random connecting, and

- Targeted connecting

Random Connecting

Random connecting is about identifying people who have already begun to engage with us and greeting them. Look at the profiles of those who leave a comment or a like on your content. See who it is who looked at our profile. If they look like someone you'd want to have a conversation with – *notice I didn't say, "Sell to"* – send them a connection request.

People who engage with your content are incredibly valuable to you. As mentioned before, as much as 50% of the content that appears in your newsfeed stems from 2nd and 3rd connections, based on interactions from your 1st connections. If someone you are not yet connected to engages with your content, connecting with them has the potential to expose your subsequent content to their network. And if they've liked something of yours in the past, it's more likely that LinkedIn, X, Facebook, or whatever social platform it's on will show them your content again.

Make a regular habit of reviewing the people who have looked at your profile. Maybe they saw something you posted or a comment you shared and they wanted to learn more about you. Maybe they searched for something, and LinkedIn thought you were the best result for that search. Either way, this provides the perfect opportunity to reach out to them, ask them, and start a dialog.

Every time anybody engages in any way with your profile or your content, 1st connection or otherwise, it's a great opportunity to ask them to have a conversation.

Our next chapter, **Be Generous**, talks more about sharing content. We share content not because we expect it to drive inbound sales traffic - it doesn't! We share it with the intention of growing our network.

Targeted Connecting

Targeted connecting involves identifying people within organizations of value to you. Prospects naturally come to mind first, but existing clients, existing and potential partners, existing and potential vendors, as well as industry leaders can also be an important part of your network. Again, it's about having more and more people knowing you for what you know.

Marketing can provide detailed insights and segmentation data regarding target audiences, helping sales reps understand who they should be connecting with and why.

Who should you intentionally connect to?

Before you send connection requests to senior leaders within an organization, you should first be connected to some people lower in the ranks within that organization. Even though you now have an incredibly compelling headline and profile, when you send a connection request to the CEO of a multinational company and you're not connected to anybody else in the organization, typically they will not accept your request - because you look like somebody that's trying to sell them something.

It's only reasonable that you do a little bit of work to get to the point where a company leader will accept a connection request from you. We need to make sure that we are connecting to several people across the ranks of an organization. Although it doesn't matter whether any one particular associate within an organization accepts your connection request, it matters that some do. Not only will being connected to several people within a company establish credibility as you reach out to the company leaders, the relationships you build with those initial connections can provide you with insight to the organization and even facilitate additional connections.

What do I say?

While efficient, if you simply send a blank connection request to as many people as you possibly can, you'll get a relatively low acceptance rate. Most people see that as a sales outreach (which it generally is) and ignore it. You cannot build a relationship without first establishing a connection.

Alternatively, when you send a highly personalized connection request, particularly if it's a friendly and slightly flattering connection request, the likelihood of them accepting the request increases significantly. The challenge with those kinds of invites is that it takes 5 to 25 minutes to compose each one, if not more. And if you're going to be sending 50 or more connection requests each week (and you should be sending at least 10 requests per day), you haven't got 25 minutes to spend composing each one. At that rate, sending connection requests would be a full-time job.

Some profiles call for a highly personalized approach, but for others a semi-personalized approach is sufficient. Not everyone is active on social media; spending time crafting a highly personalized message to someone who never sees it makes no sense. And how are you to know who is active and who is not? If they are not active on social media, they are not likely to accept your request; if they are more active, they might. Once the recipient connects with you, you can work on personalizing your future correspondence.

Like with so much else in sales and business, this is a numbers game. The more people that you connect with, the more people you can invite to have a call with. And the more people you get to know, the more people know you for what you want to be known for.

Crafting a Semi-Personalized Message

When it comes to crafting a semi-personalized message, you want to make sure it's relevant to the recipient's industry and their role. It should let them know why you reached out to connect with them and what they should expect by accepting your connection request. You can easily replicate a message like this, adding the recipient's name to the top as you go, and complete your daily outreach in 10 minutes or less.

When a Highly Personalized Message is Appropriate

With senior leaders within an organization, not only should we customize the message, but we should also do some pre-work. Look at the activity on their profile, see the things they engaged with, read the things they posted. Before connecting with them, find a meaningful way to take part in the conversations they're taking part in.

Ideally, an opportunity to start a dialogue with them will present itself. But even if no direct exchange takes place, as you both contribute to industry conversations you will be bumping into each other across

LinkedIn. This can lead to an opportunity to reach out and connect. And when you do reach out, and when you do eventually connect, remember: *There is no sales message!*

If we want to start conversations and ultimately relationships in this space, we must be significantly more subtle than that. We need to first make sure that we are building a digital bridge between us and the people that we want to forge a relationship with. And the way we do that is by having them become part of our network and us theirs.

EXERCISE: Developing Your Outreach Message

Some say to send out connection requests with no messages because you will get a better response. To them I say: Send better messages!

Creating effective outreach messages on LinkedIn requires a balance of personalization, brevity, and clarity. Here are 5 steps you can take to develop outreach messages that are more likely to receive positive responses:

Step 1. Understand Your Objective

Define Your Goal: Understand exactly why you want to connect with this person. Are you looking for job opportunities, seeking advice, looking to collaborate, or seeking to expand your base within target accounts? Your goal will shape your message.

Identify Your Audience: Understand who you're reaching out to and why they are the right people to connect with. This could be based on their industry, role, or shared interests. Tailor your message according to the type of recipient accordingly.

Step 2. Research and Personalization (sometimes)

There are times when extensive research and personalization are paramount, and there are times when basic research is sufficient. For example, if you are trying to connect with someone at your target company, it may be acceptable to use a message more generic to the industry. Alternatively, if you are trying to reach out to an organizational leader or someone in a buying role, it may make sense to take the time to make your request highly personalized.

When personalization is in order -

Review their profile: Look for details about their career path, projects they've worked on, articles they've posted or shared, and any mutual connections.

Find common ground: Identify shared interests, experiences, or mutual connections to make your message more relevant.

Step 3. Crafting the Message

Greeting: Use their name to start the message, making it more personal and engaging.

Introduction: Briefly introduce yourself. Keep it short and relevant to why you're reaching out.

Purpose: Clearly state the reason for your outreach. Be specific about what you're seeking or offering. Ideally, make it them-centric; reinforce why they should want to connect.

Be Concise and Specific: Every word counts. In fact, every character counts. Ensure your message is clear and concise, focusing on the mutual benefits of connecting.

Step 4. Follow Up

Each connection accepted deserves a follow-up. When they accept, send a thank you message. No pitch. No ask of any kind.

You do not have to respond immediately upon receiving the connection request. But you should respond within one or two business days.

Now that you are connected you not limited to 200/300 characters – but that doesn't mean you should go crazy either. Acknowledge their connection. Give them a sense of what they can expect from you now that you're connected. This won't be the last time you interact with them, so you don't have to tell them everything all at once. Simply reinforce the value you offered in the connection outreach.

Step 5. Review and Adapt

Learn from responses: Pay attention to what works and refine your approach based on the responses you receive.

Remember, the goal is to start a conversation, not to sell something right away or ask for favors. Building a relationship takes time, and your initial message is just the first step. Focus on creating a message that invites dialogue.

Example Connection Requests

[First Name],

Thank you for engaging with my recent post. I'd like to connect so that we can continue to exchange great content with each other.

Best,

Rob

[First Name],

As an enablement professional myself, I'm looking to expand my network with other professionals in enablement and share industry-related content.

Best,

Rob

[First Name],

We're both part of the Revenue Enablement Society. I thought it would be great to connect so that we can support each other.

Best,

Rob

[First Name],

Dad said you should always have a good doctor, a sharp lawyer, and an honest mechanic in your network. Might I suggest a tireless enabler too.

Anyone else you would add?

Best,

Rob

[First Name],

One of the responsibilities of sales enablement professionals is to facilitate the exchange of ideas between sales and marketing. I'd like to connect to ensure that I keep up with marketing's perspective.

Best,

Rob

[First Name],

I noticed we share an interest in enablement. I'd love to connect and exchange insights.

Best,

Rob

[First Name],

We both attended [event/conference] but we didn't meet. What were your top takeaways?

Best,

Rob

These examples aim to maintain a balance of personalization, relevance, and brevity, increasing the likelihood of a positive response.

Here are several examples of follow-up messages thanking someone for accepting a connection request:

Example Follow-Up Messages

[Name],

Thanks for connecting. I look forward to sharing insights and staying in touch.

Best,

Rob

Appreciate the connection, [Name]! Excited to learn from each other.

Best,

Rob

[Name],

Thanks for connecting. Looking forward to engaging and sharing ideas.

Best,

Rob

Great to be connected, [Name]! Looking forward to exchanging ideas.

Best,

Rob

[Name],

Thanks for connecting. I'm excited to have you in my network and look forward to engaging with your content and sharing insights.

Best,

Rob

Hi [Name],

Thanks for accepting my connection request. I'm looking forward to learning from your experiences in [industry/topic]. If there's ever an opportunity to collaborate or discuss ideas, please don't hesitate to reach out.

Best,

Rob

These follow-up messages help reinforce the connection and express a willingness to engage without immediately pitching or asking for favors.

Your Turn

Your goal is to expand your network with others in your industry.

Your target audience is people working for an organization you want to work with - a prospective client, partner, or otherwise.

Develop a semi-personalized message suitable for many within that organization.

Send connect requests to at least 10 people in that organization. **NOW!**

Chapter Six

Be Generous

Why: The Importance of Valuable and Original Content

What Do We Mean by "Be Generous?"

In his book **Jab, Jab, Jab, Right Hook** Gary V. says, "Give value. Give value. Give value. *Then* ask."

Being generous means going beyond the basics of sharing random content. And it's definitely more than posting your latest brochure or "All about me!" content. It's about contributing value to your network in a way that fosters trust, builds relationships, and positions you as a thought leader. When we talk about being generous, we emphasize the importance of giving more than you take, especially when it comes to content.

Generosity in social enablement manifests in several key ways:

Providing Valuable Insights: Sharing content that not only informs but also educates and inspires your network. This could be in the form of industry news, insightful articles, or practical tips that can be applied immediately. The goal is to offer something that your network finds genuinely useful.

Offering Unique Perspectives: Don't simply repost without comment or regurgitate what everyone else is saying. Add your own commentary and insights to the content you share. This shows that you have a deep understanding of the subject matter and are willing to contribute your expertise to the conversation.

Engaging Actively with Your Network: Being generous also means engaging with the content that others share. Comment thoughtfully, ask questions, and share your thoughts. This active participation helps build stronger relationships and shows that you are genuinely interested in what others have to say.

Facilitating Conversations: Use your content to spark discussions. Ask open-ended questions and encourage your audience to share their thoughts and experiences. This not only increases engagement but also positions you as a community leader who values the input of others.

Consistently Contributing: Regularly posting valuable content keeps you top of mind with your audience. It demonstrates that you are committed to providing ongoing value, rather than just occasional insights.

Generosity has always been a cornerstone of building meaningful and lasting relationships. In the digital age it has become incredibly easy to do so.

 Leadership can model the behavior of posting content by sharing their insights just as they would do at a team meeting.

Using Content to Facilitate Conversations

Not only is sharing valuable and original content generous, in the IGNITE methodology content is leveraged as a powerful tool to spark meaningful interactions. Rather than simply broadcasting information, we use our social media posts to initiate dialogues. Every like is an opportunity to connect with someone new. Every comment is a chance to start a dialog, both publicly and one-on-one. These triggers give you specific reasons to reach out and engage with potential or existing network connections.

When someone engages with content you've shared - whether it's an article, a blog post, a piece of industry news, or something original you created - it signals their interest in the topic. Use this trigger to initiate a conversation. For example, if someone likes or comments on a shared article, you can thank them for their input and ask for their opinion on a related issue. If they are not already a first connection, send them a connection request with the intent of continuing to exchange industry related insights. If they are already a first connection, send them a direct message inviting them to schedule a chat to talk more about the issue.

How: Determining Valuable Content to Share

Identifying your niche and the specific needs of your network is a foundational step in sharing content that resonates. While it's tempting to try to appeal to everyone, we recommend narrowing your focus and establishing yourself as an expert in a particular area.

Remember, you want people to know you for what you want to be known for. While "A jack of all trades is a master of none, but oftentimes better than a master of one," it is much easier to be known for something when that something is well-defined, even hyper-specific. For instance, rather than targeting the broad field of sales, one could focus specifically on the sub-set of sales that involves sales training or social enablement.

Finding Valuable Content

To establish our credibility, to become known for what we want to be known for, it's essential for us to consistently share valuable content. The more high-quality content we share, the more we reinforce our reputation.

When it comes to curating content, this means consistently seeking out high-quality material that aligns with your niche and resonates with your network. Ideally, you have already established a habit of "sharpening the saw" - constantly reading, learning, and keeping up with the latest topics and trends in your industry. Sharpening the saw is all about continuous improvement and preparation, and this can provide a great source of content to share with your network.

Thought leaders and industry publications are great sources of content worth sharing with your network. Business newsletters, industry-specific platforms, and Slack channels devoted to exchanging the latest thinking and views are also good sources to find content worth sharing. But don't simply limit yourself to what everyone else in your industry is reading. Draw from a wide-ranging eclectic set of sources to find content.

Another way to identify content worth sharing is to conduct keyword research to identify topics trending and relevant to your network. The easiest way to do this is through the search engine itself. For example, when you type in "sales expert" the autocomplete shows other people's previous search queries that are similar. The Google Ads Keyword Planner is a free tool that provides a ranking of keywords by search volume; it also goes beyond just looking for the exact words searched, providing a wider view of industry trends. Moz, Semrush, and Ahrefs are among additional online tools providing free keyword research.

Marketing can enable sales teams by providing access to or insights from resources already in use like the Google Ads Keyword Planner, SEO resources, and social listening tools.

With these keywords and trends in hand, leverage platforms such as X, LinkedIn, and Flipboard to follow hashtags and topics to curate diverse and engaging content. Google News and other social listening tools can be set up to listen for specific terms and deliver notifications to you when they appear online and in social media. And user-generated platforms like Reddit and Medium are excellent places to discover relevant and unique material.

Best Practices for Sharing Valuable Content

Anyone can flip a piece of content from one platform to another. However, that generally does not help you become known for what you what to be known for. And rarely will it facilitate an opportunity to have a conversation. You need to be sharing content in a way that works for you.

Add value to what you are sharing. There are a lot of great books and whitepapers providing industry insights. Yes, others in your industry may have access to the same information, but not everybody finds a chance to read them. Use this as an opportunity to give them the TL;DR. Summarize the 100+ pages in a bulleted list.

Adding commentary is another way to add value to your network. Call out a specific idea expressed and why it's important. Tell them why they should (or should not) take the time to read the article for themselves. This not only provides value to your network, it positions as a valuable resource you in terms of the topic you want to be known for.

Leadership can meaningfully engage with sales reps' content. Don't just like it, add a comment saying why you like it, what "A-ha!" you had after reading it.

By curating and enhancing the content you share, you encourage conversations and interactions. This approach ensures that your contributions are always valuable and impactful, helping you build trust and establish authority within your network. It also serves to address your primary goal - initiate conversations so that people can get to know you for what you know.

What's the 4-1-1?

Wondering how frequently you should be posting? Remember, if we're using content to drive conversations we should be trying to drive conversations every day. Consider the 4-1-1 method.

Four pieces of curated content - something interesting that you have found, generally related to your industry.

One piece of content created by you - something that you have written (we'll address content creation later in this chapter), generally business related, but not a pitch, a brochure, or a billboard for your organization.

One piece of personal content - something about you, or what you're doing, or what you love. Something that shows the human side of you. Something that makes people think, "Yeah, they're authentic, they're real. I'd like to have them in my network."

The curated content establishes that you're knowledgeable in your industry, but it doesn't demonstrate that it's your knowledge. Content created by you demonstrates your knowledge and that you have an active voice in your industry.

The last piece, the personal content is the most important. Ask anybody in sales, "What would you rather: Have a meeting in a client's office or take them to a ball game for a day?" Most would choose the ball game. Not only would you have a nice outing for the day, but you've also got an opportunity to get to know them at a more human level.

Your sharing of personal content - not private content, but personal content – something like, "I went to the beach today." Or "My passion away from work is cycling. I can't wait until I go on vacation to explore the rail trail on my new bike." Whatever it is that you're passionate about, talk about that. Because if you're passionate about it, it's likely there will be other people who are passionate about it too. And as you post about it, they are likely to engage with it. Every engagement is an opportunity to have a conversation, and every conversation is a way of getting more people to know you for what you want to be known for.

 HR can encourage members of employee communities (affinity groups, ERG, BRGs, etc.) to share their stories.

Some balk at the thought of posting personal content saying, "I'm not here to make friends," or, "I have a quota to meet," or my favorite, "This isn't Facebook!" Here's the cold, hard facts about the content you post: You are likely to get 10 times the engagement on your personal content than you are on your curated content or even the original content you create. Why? Because personal content is easy to engage with. And people like doing business with people they like.

For some, committing to posting content 6 days per week is daunting. That's understandable, but what can you commit to? Can you commit to posting 3 days per week? Maybe just 2? While the more content you share, the more opportunities you have to spark a conversation - and ultimately, a relationship - it's more important to develop a habit, even if that means growing into a more robust habit as you go along.

But the important thing is this - You need to develop a cadence that will drive the results you want. Random bits of posting only once in a while will not provide enough opportunity to drive the results you are seeking.

What: Creating Original Content

While there is no lack of content to share, creating original content is an important part of the IGNITE process. Sharing content allows you to engage with and grow your network. But creating content also allows you to stand out from the competition.

How many of your competitive peers are posting content? LinkedIn tells us that only 2% of active users post regularly (and they define posting regularly as one or more times *per month)*. And while there are no statistics around the types of content they're posting, anecdotally we know that much of our newsfeed is filled with digital brochures about their products and self-congratulatory pats on the back. Translation: there is a low bar set for creating content that is interesting and helpful to your network.

Creating your own content allows you to engage more deeply with your audience, grow your network, and distinguish yourself from the competition. Original content provides a platform to demonstrate your knowledge and insights directly.

Finally, personal and unique content is inherently more engaging. People are drawn to genuine, original perspectives. By sharing your own experiences and insights, you create content that resonates more deeply with your audience, fostering stronger connections and greater engagement. This approach not only helps you stand out but also ensures that your voice is heard amidst the sea of banality.

Leadership can provide clarity and ensure your sales team understands specifically what the organization wants to be known for and by whom. Hint: If it can't fit into a tweet (280 characters) it might not be clear enough.

Identifying Topics to Write About

Determining what to write about can often feel daunting, but it's an essential step in creating content that resonates with your audience. Did you know that every 3-meter square of the world has been given a unique combination of three words? You can find the unique 3-word combination for any location in the world at what3words.com

That's great for finding places that already exist. But what about finding places that are yet to exist, as in: *How do I find my place in the world?*

You are probably wondering how you are going to be the best in the world at your "thing" - whatever that thing may be. But you do not have to be the single best person at any one thing to find your unique place in the world.

Instead, figure out something where you would consider yourself average. Don't limit your thinking to the subset of only those who have studied the given topic. And don't necessarily limit it to something business related. Of the total world's population, where would you fall into the top 25% of people in the world when it comes to subject matter knowledge of a given topic? The world is a pretty big place - we're rapidly approaching 8 billion people on the planet. It turns out you don't have to be a genius at something - anything - to know as much as (or more than) 3 out of 4 people in the world on any given topic.

For example, what's something you could speak about for 5 minutes (or more) without advance preparation? Maybe it's a sport you play or a team you follow. Maybe it's a hobby - bike riding, reading mysteries, or maybe you're a movie buff. Maybe it's celebrity gossip - no shade, we need people to chronicle the zeitgeist of the day. Whatever it is, think of that thing.

Got that one thing? Great! Now come up with two more. And the more disparate they are from each other, the better. One could be something in your industry that you could speak about for 5 minutes or more. Again, it doesn't have to be something where you are the world's thought leader, just something where you can contribute to the conversation.

And one could be from within your organization – a pain point you hear about often from prospects and clients, a problem your company solves, whatever – something you could speak about for 5 minutes without advance preparation. What are the 3 most frequently asked questions you address when speaking with prospective clients (aside from price)?

Now, think of the intersection of your three points. That's your place! *You are in the top 2% of all people in the world who can speak to the intersection of those 3 topics.*

Want the math? If you are in the top 25% of any given subject, that means you fall within the 75th percentile - not even one full standard deviation from the exact middle. That's not "above average" - that *is* average. But in this case, average is OK.

When you are in the top 25% of two subjects, you are in the top 6.25% of the intersection of those two subjects together. And when you are in the top 25% of three subjects, **you are in the top 1.6% of everyone in the world** when it comes to the intersection of all three subjects. There's your unique place in the world.

While our goal isn't necessarily to become *the* leading authority on a topic, we do want to be recognized as a knowledgeable and trusted voice on that topic. Draw interesting parallels, especially as your "3 words" intersect.

Knowing the specific needs and challenges of your network allows you to share content that addresses their pain points directly. Share not only solutions, but don't hesitate to share your challenges and invite others' insights.

Remember, we are using content to facilitate conversations; having an interesting perspective on a topic of interest to your network is a great way to spark an opportunity to connect and schedule a call.

 Enablement can assist in the creation of a structured content calendar that outlines key dates and themes, helping sales reps plan their posts in advance and ensuring consistency in content creation.

HR can help make the organization, and thereby the people within it, more approachable by telling stories that matter. Talk about the organization's human-interest stories (philanthropy, DEI initiative, etc.) and highlight specific employees in the process.

You Do Not Want Your Post to Go Viral!

"If it's worth doing, it's worth doing right," right? Yes, you want to make sure that if you are going to put time and effort into creating content that it drives results. Tracking the metrics around your content gives you a sense of what's working and where you might want to change tack.

But by themselves, likes and views are a vanity metric and have absolutely zero value. We're publishing content to engage in conversations. Likes and views do not necessarily lead to the results we are seeking. If you have a post with 20,000 views, 500 likes, and 200 comments, you could never keep up with that onslaught. You could never initiate 700 connections and conversations. You would miss opportunities; but most would not be true opportunities.

And that makes sense because the more people who see your content, especially viral content, the further the viewers are from your ideal target audience. You cannot be both *highly specific* and *relevant to everybody*.

> We had one client have a post reach 1.6 MILLION views.
> It led to exactly ZERO conversations.
>
> A viral piece of content is great for your ego. It's lousy for your business.

Whereas if you have a post that gets 200 views, 20 likes, and 6 comments, that's very easy to leverage. You can follow up with those who liked it, inviting them to be part of your network. You can exchange comments with those who commented, and maybe even turn that into a one-on -one conversation.

This is another example of where IGNITE differs from most other social selling training programs and LinkedIn gurus. We are not here to make you a "capital 'I' Influencer"; we are here to help you drive more business opportunity.

Types of Content

As you work to establish your reputation for what you want to be known for, creating a variety of content helps you engage your network in multiple ways. From short text posts to detailed articles, each type of content serves a unique purpose.

Text posts are great for quick updates and insights, while articles allow for in-depth exploration of topics and can be pinned to your profile for lasting visibility. Visual content, like images and infographics, simplifies complex information and captures attention, whereas videos and live broadcasts showcase your personality and expertise dynamically. Interactive content like polls can foster engagement and help you understand your network better.

While the social platforms are always experimenting with new ways of engagement, here are the most common types of content you can create:

Text Posts: The most common type of post, these are short-form pieces of content that can include updates, insights, and questions to engage your network. They're ideal for quick thoughts or sharing other content. Text posts can be enhanced by including images or other media.

Articles: These are long-form content pieces that allow for in-depth exploration of topics. Google indexes LinkedIn articles for organic search results, expanding their reach beyond the platform's users. Articles can be pinned to your profile for ongoing visibility and are great for establishing expertise.

Videos: This dynamic content can be used to showcase both your personality and expertise. Videos are highly engaging and can be used for tutorials, insights, and updates.

Infographics: Infographics simplify complex information into an easily digestible format, making it engaging and informative. Done well, these are both highly informative and highly engaging.

Slide Decks (Documents): Presentations or PDF documents that can be uploaded and viewed directly on LinkedIn. These are useful for sharing detailed information, reports, and case studies.

Polls: Interactive content that allows you to ask questions and gather opinions from your network, polls can be great for engagement and understanding your network's views.

Live Events: Real-time broadcasting to your network. Live videos are highly engaging and can be used for events, Q&A sessions, and live tutorials.

By posting diverse types of content, you can engage your LinkedIn network in various ways and establish a strong, well-rounded presence on the platform.

 Marketing can assist by sharing or producing images and/or graphics that support sales reps' content.

Cross-Post Content to Maximize Reach

Once you have developed a piece of content, cross-posting it among different platforms is a strategic approach to maximizing your reach and creative efforts. You can adapt a single piece of content to fit various platforms. For example, a LinkedIn article can be summarized into a Facebook post, broken down into a series of tweets, and visually represented in an infographic for Instagram.

Different types of content perform better on different platforms. Visual content might excel on Instagram, while detailed articles might perform better on LinkedIn. Customize your content to fit the format and network of each platform. Adjust the length, style, and type of content (e.g., images, videos, articles) to match the platform's strengths. Cross-promoting allows you to tailor your content to the strengths of each platform, boosting overall engagement.

We're trying to leverage content to initiate conversations. Each platform has its own user base with unique demographics and preferences. Cross-promoting allows you to tap into these varied networks, enhancing your content's exposure and thereby increasing the potential for initiating conversations.

Enablement can provide templates for creating various types of content, such as social posts, LinkedIn articles, tweets, and infographics, as well as to help with repurposing content in multiple formats.

Importance of Consistency

By maintaining a presence across multiple platforms, you reinforce your brand - that is, who knows you for what you want to be known for. It's important to ensure your tone and messages are consistent across all platforms. This helps reinforce your identity and makes it easier for your network to recognize and remember you.

Regularly creating posts helps to build your reputation in your field. Even if you don't consider yourself an expert, the process of creating helps you develop and refine your ideas, making you more confident and competent over time. Posting original content also provides an opportunity to receive feedback, from which you can further develop your thinking.

Schedule time for content creation to maintain a habit of posting regularly. Establishing a routine for creating content ensures that you consistently contribute valuable insights to your network. By dedicating specific times for brainstorming, drafting, and refining your content, you can produce higher quality posts without feeling rushed. Moreover, regular scheduling helps you stay disciplined and committed to your content strategy.

Surely you can set aside one hour per week for composing your content for the week and 15 minutes per day for the actual posting and responding to others' comments on your previous content. Over time, this disciplined approach will enhance your credibility and influence within your field.

Still not sure what exactly to say? Try the following exercise.

EXERCISE: Content Creation Matrix

A system for developing content ideas

Justin Welsh describes 8 content formats:

1. X vs Y: Comparing two things

2. Listicle: Listed points, e.g. '5 Best Ways to...' or 'Top 9 Reasons for...'

3. Observation: Simply sharing an observation

4. Motivational: Motivation related to your niche

5. Actionable: Teach people how to do something

6. Analytical: Explain something and use data to support your position

7. Contrarian: Say something that is against the grain

8. Present vs Future: Way we do something today vs future

He then suggests creating a matrix where one axis consists of the content formats and the other axis is made up of the topics you write about.

Now that you have your "3 Words", you have 7 possible topics.

1. 1st thing you can speak about for 5 minutes or more (the personal thing)

2. 2nd thing you can speak about for 5 minutes or more (the industry thing)

3. The intersection of 1 & 2

4. The 3rd thing you can speak about for 5 minutes or more (the company thing)

5. The intersection of 1 & 3

6. The intersection of 2 & 3

7. The intersection of 1, 2 & 3

For my "3 Words" (teaching, sales training, and social enablement) that might look like -

- An observation and the intersection of 1 & 2 -
  What Teaching In The Classroom Taught Me About Being a Better Sales Trainer

- A contrarian view of 2 -
  Sales Training Is Not The Waste of Time Many Say It Is

- X vs Y and the intersection of 2 & 3 -
  The Difference Between Sales Training and Social Enablement

Coming up with what to say will be relatively easy for me. These are all things I could speak about for 5 minutes or more with no advanced preparation. It was determining what to write about in the first place that provided the real challenge.

Determining what to write about is as easy as filling out a matrix (like the one here) where the X-axis lists content formats and the Y-axis lists topics.

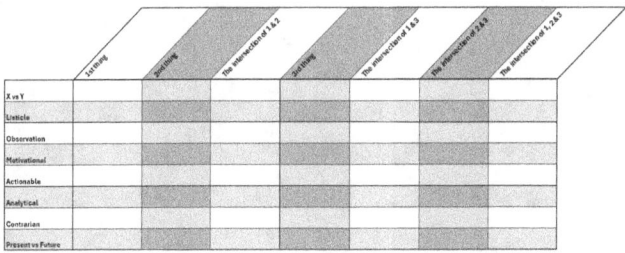

Now you try it!

Develop a list of 5 topics you can write about by using this matrix and your "3 Words".

As an added bonus: Use your keyword research to help you come up with the topics and headlines.

Chapter Seven

The Keys To Social Enablement Success

The keys to social enablement success lie in mastering the essential principles that drive effective engagement and relationship-building in the digital age. Being approachable, being sociable, and being generous are the keys not only to sales success, but also to building lasting professional relationships, fostering trust within your network, and establishing yourself as a thought leader in your industry.

Always Be Connecting is the modern mantra for sales professionals, emphasizing the continuous effort to build and nurture relationships rather than just focusing on closing deals. Ongoing engagement is crucial for staying top of mind and expanding your professional network. Leveraging social media platforms effectively allows you to interact with a diverse audience, share your expertise, and demonstrate thought leadership, thereby increasing your visibility and credibility.

Consistency is critical for maintaining a strong social presence. And focusing on progress rather than perfection is essential in the fast-paced world of social media. Each interaction and piece of content becomes an opportunity for learning and refinement, contributing to your overall strategy and success.

By incorporating these principles and maintaining a strategic approach, you can achieve significant success in social enablement. This comprehensive and integrated effort not only attracts interest and builds meaningful connections but also provides ongoing value to your network, ensuring sustained success in a social-first business landscape.

Recap of the IGNITE Methodology

The IGNITE methodology is built on three core principles that are essential for creating a robust social enablement strategy: **Be Approachable**, **Be Sociable**, and **Be Generous**.

Be Approachable

Being approachable starts with managing your digital presence. This means crafting a professional and engaging profile on platforms like LinkedIn. Your profile is often the first impression potential clients and connections will have of you, so it's crucial to make it count. Highlight your expertise, use relevant keywords, and ensure your profile picture and background image are professional and inviting. An approachable online persona invites conversations and opportunities, making it easier for others to reach out and connect with you.

Be Sociable

Being sociable goes beyond merely being present on social media; it involves actively engaging with your network. This means not only connecting with people but also interacting with their content, sharing valuable insights, and participating in meaningful conversations. Building and nurturing your network requires consistent effort. By being sociable, you foster relationships that can lead to new opportunities, collaborations, and business growth. Authentic engagement helps you stay top of mind and build a reputation as a valuable and trusted connection.

Be Generous

Generosity in the context of social enablement means sharing your knowledge, insights, and resources freely. This could be through writing informative articles, creating helpful content, or simply offering advice and support to your network. Being generous with your expertise establishes you as a thought leader and trusted advisor in your field. It builds goodwill and encourages others to reciprocate, further strengthening your professional relationships. The more value you provide to your network, the more you will be seen as an indispensable resource.

Together, these principles create a powerful framework for social enablement. By being approachable, you attract interest. By being sociable, you build meaningful connections. By being generous, you provide ongoing value that cements your status as a key player in your field. This integrated approach ensures that your social enablement efforts are effective, sustainable, and beneficial for both you and your network.

Always Be Connecting

The classic ABCs of selling, famously articulated in the movie **Glengarry Glen Ross**, emphasized a hard-nosed approach to sales: "Always Be Closing." This mantra represented a relentless focus on pushing for the sale above all else. However, in today's social-first business environment, this approach is not only outdated but also counterproductive.

Dan Pink, in his book **To Sell Is Human**, redefines the ABCs for modern sales: Attunement, Buoyancy, and Clarity. These principles focus on understanding the perspective of others, maintaining a positive outlook, and clearly communicating your value proposition. While these principles are crucial, the rapid evolution of social media and digital networking demands an additional shift: **Always Be Connecting**.

Always Be Connecting is the new mantra for sales professionals in the digital age. This principle emphasizes the importance of continuously building and nurturing relationships rather than solely focusing on closing deals. Here's why it's essential:

Building Genuine Relationships: In a world where buyers are more informed and have access to endless information, building genuine relationships is key. By connecting with your network regularly, you create a foundation of trust and mutual respect, which is far more valuable than a single transaction.

Expanding Your Network: Regularly connecting with new people expands your professional network, increasing your reach and influence. This expansion opens doors to new opportunities, insights, and potential collaborations that you might not have encountered otherwise.

Staying Top of Mind: Consistent engagement keeps you on the radar of your connections. Whether it's through sharing valuable content, commenting on posts, or simply reaching out to say hello, these small actions ensure that you remain a relevant and valuable contact within your network.

Leveraging Social Media: Platforms like LinkedIn, X, and others are powerful tools for staying connected. They allow you to interact with a diverse audience, share your expertise, and demonstrate thought leadership. By actively participating in these platforms, you enhance your visibility and credibility.

Creating Value: Always Be Connecting is not just about increasing numbers; it's about creating value. Each interaction should aim to provide something beneficial to the other party, whether it's information, support, or inspiration. This value-centric approach fosters deeper connections and long-term loyalty.

By embracing the new ABCs - Always Be Connecting - you transform your approach to sales and networking. This principle aligns perfectly with the IGNITE methodology, reinforcing the importance of being approachable, sociable, and generous. It ensures that your professional relationships are not just transactional but transformational, leading to sustained success in the social-first business landscape.

Consistency is Key

Consistency is the cornerstone of any successful social enablement strategy. In the fast-paced world of social media, where trends and conversations evolve rapidly, maintaining a regular and consistent presence is crucial. It's not enough to simply make a strong initial impression; you must continually reinforce your presence to remain relevant and top of mind for your audience.

By consistently engaging with your network, sharing valuable content, and participating in conversations, you build a reliable and trustworthy image. This steady activity helps to establish you as an authority in your field, as someone who is committed and dependable. Over time, this builds credibility and fosters trust among your connections.

However, maintaining consistency can be challenging, especially when balancing it with other professional responsibilities. Start by setting achievable goals for your social media activity. Rather than aiming to post every day, which can be daunting, begin with a manageable schedule, such as three times a week. As you become more comfortable, you can gradually increase your activity.

Plan your content in advance. Set time aside to create a number of content pieces and use a content calendar to plan when to share your posts in advance. Don't be afraid to repurpose your existing content. A well-received post can be broken down into a series of tweets. Similarly, a webinar and podcast appearances can be edited into short clips for sharing. Repurposing content saves time and ensures that you get the most mileage out of your efforts.

Consistency isn't just about posting regularly; it's also about engaging with your audience. Make it a habit to participate in discussions, interact with your connections' posts, and respond to comments. This two-way engagement strengthens your relationships and enhances your visibility.

Progress Over Perfection

The journey of social enablement is one of ongoing development. The fast-paced nature of social media and digital interactions means that waiting for the perfect moment, the perfect post, or the perfect strategy can result in missed opportunities. Instead, adopt a mindset focused on progress rather than perfection. Embrace a philosophy of continuous improvement. This is a lot less daunting and allows you to begin, make steady advances, and achieve meaningful results over time.

The social media landscape is constantly evolving, with new trends, tools, and platforms emerging regularly. By focusing on progress, you also allow yourself the flexibility to experiment, learn, and adapt. Each interaction, post, or appearance becomes a learning opportunity, contributing to your growth and the refinement of your strategy.

Time to Take Action

To implement the IGNITE methodology effectively, it's crucial to transition from theory to practice with concrete action steps. Begin by evaluating your current social media presence. Take a thorough look at your profiles on platforms like LinkedIn, X, and Facebook, ensuring they reflect a professional and approachable image. Update your profiles with relevant keywords, a professional photo, and a clear, compelling summary that highlights your expertise and value proposition.

Once your profiles are polished, the next step is to start building and nurturing your network. Reach out to colleagues, industry peers, and potential clients, inviting them to connect. When sending connection requests, personalize your messages to explain why you want to connect and how you can add value to their network. This personal touch sets the stage for meaningful interactions and stronger relationships.

Begin sharing valuable content regularly. These could be articles, insights, or industry news that your network will find useful. Create a content calendar to help you plan and maintain a consistent posting schedule. Don't just focus on quantity; ensure that your posts provide genuine value to your audience, establishing you as a thought leader in your field.

Engagement is key to the IGNITE methodology. Actively participate in conversations by commenting on posts, asking questions, and sharing your insights. This not only increases your visibility but also demonstrates your expertise and willingness to engage with others. Additionally, don't shy away from initiating discussions on topics relevant to your industry. This proactive approach can help you build a reputation as a knowledgeable and influential figure within your professional community.

To further solidify your social presence, consider creating original content such as posts, videos, or podcasts. Share your unique perspectives and experiences and encourage feedback and discussions. This not only enhances your credibility but also fosters a deeper connection with your network.

Are you ready to implement a social enablement program in your organization?

Social enablement is not just a shift in tools or tactics; it represents a comprehensive transformation in how your organization engages with potential clients, potential employees, and the public at large. For those advocating for and responsible for establishing a formal, strategic social enablement training program, it's crucial to assess your readiness and outline a clear implementation plan.

Begin by evaluating your current sales and marketing practices. Conduct a thorough review to identify what's working, what's not, and where there are opportunities for integrating social enablement. Understand the social presence of each person on your team or in your organization.

Understanding your audience is equally important. Analyze their behaviors and preferences on social media to tailor your approach effectively to meet their needs. But don't say that your target audience is not on social media; as we saw at the onset 3 out of 4 people in the world can be found there.

Next, present a compelling business case to your Leadership team. Clearly articulate the benefits of social enablement, highlighting how it aligns with the organization's goals and the potential return on investment. Sharing success stories from other organizations that have successfully implemented social enablement programs can help illustrate the positive outcomes and further persuade Leadership.

With Leadership on board, define clear objectives for your social enablement program. Set specific, measurable goals, such as increased engagement, lead generation, better recruitment and retention, and improved customer relationships. Create a detailed roadmap outlining the key steps and milestones for implementation, including timelines, resource allocation, and responsibilities for each stage. Most importantly, Leadership should be prepared to lead the initiative by modeling the behavior.

Identify the key roles needed and each of their specific responsibilities to drive the social enablement initiative. Ensure your team is well-equipped with the necessary skills and knowledge by investing in comprehensive training programs that cover the fundamentals of social enablement, platform-specific strategies, and advanced techniques.

Encourage your team to actively engage on social media by recognizing and rewarding contributions to the program's success. Promote collaboration between sales, marketing, and other departments to ensure a unified approach to social enablement.

The Case for Social Enablement

As with any significant shift in strategy, the idea of implementing social enablement can be met with resistance. Many sales professionals and leaders may express skepticism about social enablement, feeling that their teams are already busy with traditional sales methods and meeting their targets. They might question the need to invest time and resources into something new and seemingly unproven. Concerns typically include the learning curve, the time investment, and uncertainty about the return on investment.

However, it's important to understand that social enablement is not just another trend; it's a necessary evolution in the approach to sales. Buyers today are more informed and prefer to research solutions independently before engaging with sales representatives. Studies show that a significant portion of the buyer's journey is completed before they ever speak to a salesperson. By adopting social enablement, we meet buyers where they are, providing valuable insights and building relationships earlier in their journey. This positions us as trusted advisors, not just vendors.

As more companies adopt social selling strategies, those who stick solely to traditional methods risk falling behind. Embracing social enablement ensures we remain competitive in a rapidly evolving market. Investing in social enablement training is an investment in your future, equipping your organization with the skills and strategies needed to stay ahead of competitors and thrive in a digital-first business environment.

Chapter Eight

Social Enablement Beyond Sales

While earlier in the book we introduced Five Key Benefits of the IGNITE Methodology, our discussion so far has primarily focused on driving pipeline growth and empowering Sales Teams to connect with prospects and clients more effectively. However, the potential of social enablement extends far beyond Sales.

Social enablement is a crucial component of organizational digital transformation, offering numerous benefits across various departments and roles. The following highlights eight other parts of an organization, both customer-facing and non-customer-facing, that can leverage social enablement for the organization's benefit.

The benefits of social enablement also extend to **Job Seekers** and **Students**. Insights on how social enablement can help them will also be shared.

Leadership

Even as a leader in your organization, you don't have to be a "capital 'I' Influencer" to leverage social media. Maybe you don't want to be a "capital 'I' Influencer." But if you are in a leadership role, you are most certainly a voice of influence within your organization.

Value to Your Employees

If you are a voice of influence within your organization, it stands to reason that you could share your voice beyond that of your organization. If you have lessons to share with the next generation of leadership within your organization, it's highly likely that there are people in other organizations who could benefit from hearing what you have to say.

According to Apollo Technical, a technical staffing company, "83% of businesses say it's important to develop leaders at all levels, yet less than 5% of companies have implemented leadership development across all levels." For so many aspiring leaders, they are not getting guidance on leadership from anyone. But they are seeking it.

- **Mentorship and Development:** Your insights can serve as valuable mentorship for employees, fostering a culture of continuous learning and growth.

- **Building Trust and Transparency:** Regular communication on social media can build trust within your team by showing transparency and openness.

Value to the Organization

Earlier, we discussed how startup organizations with CEOs who are active on X receive average valuations that are 5% higher than similar organizations. CEOs in startups who are active on LinkedIn average 20% more! Knowing this, to not be active on social media would be a disservice to your organization, your employees, and your investors.

Why would you not be active on social media? Maybe because you thought it was hard or didn't see any value in it. Possibly because you thought it was time-consuming. How are you spending your time if not in the interest of adding to the value of your organization? Can you tell me of any other activity that takes as little as 15 minutes per day and can add as much as 20% value to the entire organization?

- **Brand Enhancement:** An active social media presence can significantly enhance your company's brand, making it more attractive to potential clients and partners.

- **Recruitment Advantage:** Sharing your vision and company culture can attract top talent who align with your values and mission.

Make no mistake about it – an active social presence from a leader is not simply flipping Marketing's latest brochure or sharing the latest product release. It's obvious which organizations have leaders with an active social presence and the positive attitude many people have towards them and the organizations they represent. Many of these active leaders have developed loyal followers, even raving fans. Yes, some have even become Influencers.

Marketing

At first social enablement might seem daunting or even threatening to marketers. It's a shift from the traditional approach that has always been a part of marketing. However, social enablement is not about replacing the Marketing Department; it's about enhancing their role.

Value of a Personal Network in Marketing

Marketing typically involves a one-to-many broadcast of a message to build a corporate brand. Social enablement is about one-to-one conversations and building personal relationships. Marketers work hard to build awareness of the brands they represent, but seldom do they work on promoting themselves personally.

While building the company brand is essential, there is significant value in building a personal network. As a marketer, establishing personal connections can enhance your credibility and influence within the industry. When you engage in meaningful one-on-one interactions, you create a network of advocates who trust you and, by extension, the brand you represent.

Marketing Strategies and Social Enablement

Another important aspect of Marketing is to monitor the mood of the marketplace and bring those insights back to the rest of the organization. Social enablement involves gathering these insights firsthand. Traditional marketing methods often rely on broad surveys and indirect feedback, which can miss the subtle shifts and nuances of audience sentiment, crucial for creating effective marketing strategies.

Social enablement allows marketers to gather real-time feedback and insights from your network. Imagine being able to reach out to industry leaders directly and engaging in conversations that matter. These insights can be invaluable for shaping marketing strategies, as they reflect the genuine thoughts and needs of your audience. When you actively listen and engage with your network, you can adapt your campaigns to better meet their expectations and preferences.

- **Enhanced Credibility:** Building a personal network enhances your credibility and influence, which can indirectly boost the company's reputation.

- **Direct Engagement:** Engaging directly with your network allows you to gather real-time feedback and insights, helping you fine-tune your marketing strategies.

Social enablement doesn't mean abandoning traditional marketing methods. It's about enhancing those efforts by integrating new strategies in order to create a more holistic approach better aligned with today's buyers.

Client Success

Client Success teams have one of the closest relationships with an organization's customers. However, many do not fully leverage this connection. Through social enablement, Client Success can engage with customers on social media and build a community around the brand. This can significantly enhance customer relationships, loyalty, and retention.

Engaging Customers on Social Media

Engaging with customers on social media platforms can strengthen relationships and foster loyalty. When Client Success teams actively participate in social conversations, respond to customer inquiries, and share valuable content, they demonstrate a commitment to the customer's success. This one-on-one interaction helps to humanize the brand and builds trust, making customers feel valued and appreciated.

Regularly sharing insights, best practices, and success stories can provide customers with the tools and knowledge they need to succeed. By responding promptly to customer queries on social media, Client Success teams can resolve issues quickly and effectively, enhancing the overall customer experience.

Building a Community Around the Brand

Building a community around the brand involves creating spaces where customers can connect, share experiences, and support one another. Social media groups, forums, and online communities offer customers a platform to engage with both the brand and fellow users. This sense of community fosters loyalty and encourages customers to become brand advocates.

Client Success teams can facilitate these interactions by hosting webinars, live Q&A sessions, and online workshops. These events provide opportunities for customers to learn, ask questions, and interact directly with the brand and other users. Additionally, highlighting customer achievements and sharing user-generated content can create a sense of belonging and appreciation.

- **Strengthened Relationships:** Engaging with customers on social media strengthens relationships and fosters loyalty by demonstrating a commitment to their success.

- **Community Building:** Creating a community around the brand provides customers with a platform to connect, share experiences, and support one another, enhancing loyalty and advocacy.

By integrating social enablement strategies into their efforts, Client Success teams can create a more engaged and loyal customer base. This proactive approach not only improves customer retention but also helps build a strong, supportive community around the brand.

HR

Social enablement for HR has two areas of opportunity: Talent Acquisition and Employee Engagement.

Social Enablement for Recruitment

One of the main responsibilities of HR is to recruit talent. Recruiting is expensive, time-consuming, and often inaccurate. Frankly, it's broken in many organizations. But what if you never had to post another job listing again? How can social enablement help with that?

Recruiting can be transformed through social enablement. Imagine your organization being known for what it stands for, the benefits it provides, and its company culture. If people strive to work at your organization because of its reputation, you will have candidates who have been on your radar long before a role opens. These individuals will be interested in working for you because they understand and appreciate your organization, all thanks to your social enablement efforts. This approach turns recruitment from a reactive process into a proactive one.

- **Enhanced Employer Brand:** By actively showcasing your company's culture, values, and benefits on social media, you create a compelling employer brand that attracts top talent.

- **Talent Pipeline Development:** Engaging with professionals on social platforms allows you to create a talent pool of interested and qualified candidates.

Employee Engagement and Social Enablement

By being active on social media, you not only have an opportunity to become an employer of choice to future employees but help improve employee engagement with existing ones.

Employee engagement refers to the emotional commitment an employee has towards their organization and its goals. It's more than just job satisfaction; it encompasses an employee's enthusiasm, dedication, and willingness to go above and beyond their job duties.

According to Haiilo, a software company addressing Employee Engagement issues:

- 85% of employees are not engaged in the workplace

- 73% of employees are considering leaving their jobs

- Low employee engagement costs companies $450-500 billion each year

- **Companies with highly engaged workforce are 21% more profitable**

By integrating social enablement strategies into your HR practices, you can create a more engaging, supportive, and productive work environment. This not only enhances the overall employee experience but also contributes to the long-term success and profitability of your organization.

Product Development

Social enablement in Product Development offers a transformative approach to creating innovative, market-ready products. By leveraging social media, Product Development teams can enhance collaboration, gather real-time feedback, and stay ahead of industry trends.

Enhanced Collaboration and Innovation

Engaging with customers, industry experts, and other stakeholders on social media can provide a wealth of ideas and insights for new products or improvements. Actively seeking input from a wide range of voices can lead to breakthrough ideas and more robust product features. Involving customers in the product development process through social engagement can result in products that better meet user needs and foster a sense of ownership and loyalty among customers. This crowdsourcing approach taps into a diverse pool of creativity and expertise, allowing for more innovative solutions.

Real-Time Feedback and Market Validation

Social enablement allows Product Development teams to gather real-time feedback from users, which is invaluable for making informed decisions and validating market needs. Engaging with users on social media provides immediate and honest feedback about current products and potential features, guiding development in the right direction. This direct engagement helps ensure that products are designed and refined based on actual user experiences and preferences.

Competitive Analysis and Trend Monitoring

Monitoring social media for emerging trends and competitor activities helps Product Development teams stay ahead of the curve. Keeping a pulse on social media trends ensures that Product teams are aware of the latest developments and consumer preferences. Understanding what competitors are doing and what the market is looking for can inform strategic decisions and drive innovation. Being active on social media allows Product teams to quickly adapt to changes in the market, ensuring that the product portfolio remains relevant and competitive.

- **Accelerated Innovation:** Leveraging social media for collaboration and feedback accelerates the development of innovative products, ensuring they meet market needs effectively.

- **Enhanced Market Position:** Monitoring trends and competitor activities on social media helps Product Development teams stay competitive and adapt quickly to market changes.

By leveraging social media for engagement, feedback, and trend monitoring, product development teams can create products that better meet customer needs and stay ahead of competitors. This proactive approach not only accelerates development cycles but also enhances the overall success and competitiveness of the organization.

Engineering

Engineers play a critical role in driving innovation and technological advancement within an organization. Leveraging social enablement can significantly enhance their innovative impact.

Innovation Sharing

Innovation sharing is a powerful tool for engineers to establish themselves and their organization as thought leaders. By actively sharing insights about new technologies, processes, and innovations on social platforms, engineers can demonstrate their expertise and the cutting-edge work being done within the organization.

Sharing innovations not only positions engineers as leaders in their field but also attracts potential clients and top talent. Talented professionals are drawn to companies known for their innovation and leadership. By showcasing the latest projects and technological advancements, the organization becomes a magnet for high-quality candidates looking to work with industry leaders.

Furthermore, regularly showcasing innovations enhances the organization's reputation. It signals to customers, stakeholders, and the broader industry that the company is at the forefront of technological advancement, driving trust and credibility.

Community Engagement

Engaging with the engineering community is another crucial aspect of social enablement. By participating in online forums and communities related to their field, engineers can exchange knowledge, troubleshoot problems, and stay updated on the latest industry trends.

Building professional networks through community engagement also opens up opportunities for collaboration and recruitment. Moreover, staying engaged with the community ensures that engineers remain informed about the latest trends and technologies. This keeps the organization competitive and adaptable in a rapidly changing industry landscape.

- **Enhanced Reputation:** Sharing innovations and participating in industry communities enhances the organization's reputation as a leader in technological advancement.

- **Continuous Learning:** Engaging with the engineering community fosters a culture of continuous learning and improvement, keeping the organization competitive.

By integrating social enablement strategies into their efforts, engineers can drive innovation, build strong professional networks, and contribute to the organization's success. This proactive approach not only enhances their impact but also helps establish a culture of collaboration and continuous improvement.

Purchasing

In today's competitive market, purchasing professionals must leverage every tool available to optimize their operations. Building stronger networks is an effective way of doing so. Social enablement in Purchasing enhances supplier relationships, market intelligence, brand reputation, and operational efficiency.

Engagement and Communication

Actively engaging with suppliers on social media platforms can significantly strengthen relationships. Open communication channels lead to more collaborative partnerships, better negotiation outcomes, and improved supplier performance. By sharing updates, insights, and feedback regularly, Purchasing professionals can keep suppliers aligned with their goals and expectations. And publicly acknowledging and celebrating successful partnerships on social media can foster goodwill and loyalty among suppliers. This engagement not only builds trust but also creates a more transparent and cooperative supply chain environment.

Professional Networks

Building a robust network of industry contacts through social media can open up new opportunities for collaboration, partnerships, and sourcing alternatives. By connecting with peers and industry leaders, Purchasing professionals can gain valuable insights and stay informed about the latest trends and innovations. Strong relationships and open communication with suppliers can lead to better negotiation outcomes, potentially reducing costs and improving terms. And engaging with suppliers and stakeholders through social media can streamline communication and procurement processes, leading to greater efficiency. By sharing insights and best practices within these networks, purchasing professionals can continuously improve their strategies and stay ahead of industry trends.

- **Enhanced Supplier Relationships:** Actively engaging with suppliers fosters stronger, more collaborative partnerships.

- **Improved Negotiation Outcomes:** Open communication and strong relationships can lead to better negotiation outcomes and cost reductions.

- **Streamlined Processes:** Leveraging social media for communication with suppliers can streamline procurement processes and enhance efficiency.

By leveraging social media for engagement, communication, and collaboration, purchasing professionals can drive significant value and contribute to the overall success of the organization. This proactive approach not only enhances operational efficiency but also strengthens the organization's market position and reputation.

Accounting

Social enablement in accounting can transform the way accountants engage with stakeholders and clients, enhancing professional credibility and building stronger relationships.

Enhancing Professional Credibility and Trust

Establishing accountants as thought leaders is a powerful way to build credibility and trust. For an accountant at a hardware manufacturer, for example, this means sharing insights on cost management, supply chain optimization, and industry trends relevant to manufacturing. By discussing these topics on social media, accountants can demonstrate their expertise and keep stakeholders informed about important developments.

"But I can't reveal financially sensitive information publicly!" It's important to note that social enablement doesn't require sharing confidential data. Instead, it involves discussing general trends, best practices, and non-sensitive insights that showcase expertise without compromising confidentiality. For instance, discussing strategies for effective cost control or the impact of market trends on raw material prices can be very informative without disclosing specific financial details.

Regularly engaging with stakeholders through social media helps to create an open dialogue, fostering a sense of trust and reliability. This transparency is crucial for maintaining the integrity of the accounting function and reinforcing the organization's commitment to ethical and effective financial practices.

Improving Client Relationships

Engaging with clients and suppliers on social media can significantly strengthen relationships and enhance satisfaction. Regular interaction through updates, answering questions, and providing financial insights helps maintain a proactive and stakeholder-centric approach. By using social media to educate clients and suppliers about financial management, cost-saving opportunities, and compliance issues, accountants add significant value to these relationships.

- **Building Credibility:** Sharing expert opinions and insights on social media enhances professional credibility and establishes accountants as thought leaders within their respective industry.

- **Strengthening Stakeholder Engagement:** Regular interaction with clients and suppliers through social media fosters a proactive and stakeholder-centric approach, improving satisfaction and loyalty.

By integrating social enablement strategies, accountants can drive significant value and contribute to the overall success of the organization. This proactive approach not only enhances the credibility and influence of the accounting function but also supports the organization's strategic goals and growth.

Job Seekers

By some accounts, between 60% and 90% of all job openings are filled through networking. If as many as 9 out of 10 jobs are filled because of who knows you for what you know, why do we spend so much time on resumes and cover letters? The reason is simple: tweaking resumes and writing cover letters is all most of us are trained to do.

The Value of Social Enablement for Job Seekers

With so much competition in traditional job-seeking methods, why not focus on how 90% of jobs are filled? Why not work on who knows you for what you know?

Much like social enablement for sales, social enablement for job seekers is not about connecting and pitching. Yes, you'll want to connect with hiring managers, if possible. But here's an even better approach: What if instead of connecting with one person at the organization where you're applying for a job, you were connected with ten or twenty? What if any one of those twenty people expressed a willingness to have a coffee chat, an informational interview, with you?

We teach students about the informational interview, but this practice need not be limited to students. When you reach out to someone in your network and request an informational interview you are not asking them for a job. You're simply asking for 15 minutes to get their insights on what it's like to work at their organization, in their role, or in their industry. If you are a knowledgeable voice in your industry and your social presence depicts you as someone worth knowing, you can leverage this to get to know more people - and have them get to know you for what you know.

Career Advancement through Social Enablement

Whether you are currently open to work, casually looking, or not considering anything at all, the more people who know you for what you know, the more opportunities will come your way. Serendipity, or luck, is the intersection of opportunity and preparation. You cannot control opportunity - it's random - but you can influence it. You can influence it with preparation and outreach. The more proactively you pursue social enablement practices, the more opportunities will find you.

- **Building Relationships:** Starting your networking efforts early and consistently allows you to build a meaningful network that can provide mentorship, advice, and job leads when you need them.

- **Expanding Opportunities:** A large and diverse network increases your chances of finding the right job. Even if your immediate connections aren't hiring, they can introduce you to others who might have opportunities.

By integrating social enablement strategies into your job search - or even *prior* to your job search - you can create a strong professional network that supports you throughout your career journey. This proactive approach not only enhances your job prospects but also helps you establish a professional identity that attracts opportunities when you aren't even looking.

Students

As an adjunct professor, I love talking to my students about career preparation. I tell them time and again that as students, they are in the best time of their LinkedIn lives. Sadly, most students don't recognize the opportunity until it's too late.

The Value of Social Enablement for Students

The value of networking as a student cannot be overstated. As a student, when you reach out to connect with someone on LinkedIn - whether it's an alumnus or someone in the industry you're studying - there's a high likelihood your request will be accepted. Most professionals can relate to being a student, and many are happy to connect with you.

Imagine if in your freshman year you sent out ten connection requests each day, 50 per week. At an 80% acceptance rate (not unreasonable for outreach targeted to alumni and professionals in your area of study), that's 40 new connections each week. That could easily translate to over 2,000 connections in a year, 8,000 connections by the time you graduate. (Even half that, 4,000 connections, is still 4X greater than the average LinkedIn user who has 930 connections.)

However students, take heed! The day you walk across the stage to receive your diploma in one hand and an offer letter in the other, the day you update your LinkedIn profile from "student" to "employee at", your LinkedIn world shifts dramatically. Suddenly, many of those once readily accepted connection requests get ignored or declined. Why not build a solid network foundation *before* you need it?

Career Preparation through Social Enablement

Building a rich and diverse network during your college years can significantly boost your career opportunities when you enter the job market. Having 8,000 connections means a vast number of people know you for what you want to be known for (i.e. your major). Because they know you, they are likely more willing to help you with your job search. They may not be able to hire you directly, but often they can facilitate introductions within their companies or within their networks.

- **Early Networking:** Starting your networking efforts early in your college career allows you to build a substantial and meaningful network. This network can provide mentorship, advice, and job leads long before you need a job.

- **Increased Opportunities:** A large network increases your chances of finding the right job. Even if your immediate connections aren't hiring, they can introduce you to others in their network who might have opportunities.

By integrating social enablement strategies into your college life, you can create a strong professional network that will support you throughout your career journey. This proactive approach not only enhances your job prospects but also helps you establish a professional identity early on.

In Conclusion

By embracing social enablement across all departments, organizations can undergo a comprehensive digital transformation to excel in this social-first world. This holistic approach not only enhances individual and departmental performance but also drives the overall growth and success of the organization. Social enablement is not just a sales tool; it is a vital strategy for empowering every part of the organization to thrive in the digital age.

Connecting With The Author

T he journey of social enablement is ongoing, and having access to additional support and coaching can significantly enhance your progress and that of your organization.

As a teacher at my core, I am committed to your success. I am always willing to share my experience and insights to help you navigate the world of social enablement.

Learn more about Social Enablement and IGNITE Social Selling & Influence training at:
https://SocialEnablement.Pro

You can reach me at:
Rob@SocialEnablement.Pro

You can connect with me at:
https://www.LinkedIn.com/in/RobDurant